COLLECTING MOMENTS:

A Guide to Retro Journaling

Lin Deng

SendPoints

COLLECTING MOMENTS:
A Guide to Retro Journaling

Originally Published by CHINA MACHINE PRESS Under the Title XIANGEI SHIGUANG DE SHOUZHANG.

Copyright © 2018 CHINA MACHINE PRESS

English Edition © 2020 Sendpoints IPS Co.,Ltd

First printing of the first edition, January 2020

SendPoints

PUBLISHED BY Sendpoints IPS Co.,Ltd

PUBLISHER: Lin Gengli

LEAD EDITOR: Lin Qiumei

EXECUTIVE EDITOR: Alice Wu

EXECUTIVE ART EDITOR: Dean Ho

REGISTERED ADDRESS: Flat/Rm 4,5/F,Tak Lee Building,270-280 Queens Road West Hongkong

TEL: +852-69502452 / **FAX:** +852-35832448

OFFICE ADDRESS: 7F, 9-1 Anning Street, Jinshazhou, Baiyun District, Guangzhou, China

TEL: +86-20-89095121 / **FAX:** +86-20-89095206

BEIJING OFFICE: Flat 1701, Block C, BBMG International, Wangjing West Road no.48, Chaoyang District, Beijing, China

TEL: +86-10-84139071 / **FAX:** +86-10-84139071

SHANGHAI OFFICE: Room 302, Floor 3, Ningbo Road no.349, Huangpu District, Shanghai, China

TEL: +86-21-63523469 / **FAX:** +86-21-63523469

SALES TEAM:

UK, Europe, Africa, Oceania: Sunnie sales02@sendpoints.cn

America, the Middle East: Mia sales03@sendpoints.cn

Asia: Hedy sales01@sendpoints.cn

TEL: +86-20-81007895

WEBSITE: www.sendpoints.cn / www.spbooks.cn

ISBN 978-988-74067-1-6

Lin Deng, the author of this book in the original Chinese version is a toy designer and the founder of Mosswood Stationery Design Studio. The exquisite and retro style of her art journals wins the affection of everyone who loves doing handwork.

Defending the home front.
Poiret influence was still apparent
in the 1910s. His designs sparked a fad for hobble
skirts in the World Seated, as American dress-
makers misinterpreted the narrow lines of
designer's look.

PART BY THE MASSIVE IMMIGRATION IN
DECADE.

...ricans in the 1910s took an isolationists nativist
...and nostalgia for small-town living began to
grow. Meanwhile,
discent was brewing
abroad. within a few
years. Europe and
soon ness. Chicago
based men's apparel
manufacturer
and
retailer.
B...
...pa...ion
Co.
...was any
of another
apparel market
and retailer
Society
Brand
Clothing. looked to
the allies and

17. 11. 11
123456...

THIS IS THE IDEAL LIFE.

the newly decommissioned fighter
planes and pilots — to pioneer a new
means of distribution for his products.
Air delivery.

Into the midst of growing international
conflict. Gabrielle "Coco" Chanel opened a
hat shop in Paris, followed shortly by
dress shop in Deauville and Biarritz
where she began using wool
jersey, a fabric previously
used for men's underwear
to create comfortable.
chic. modern women's
apparel. Chanel's
was a departure
from booth.
the corseted
Gibson Girl
of the first
decade.

Gibson Girl

In 1907. Australian swimming star Annette
Kellerman performed the first water ballet
at New York's Hippodrome. Her one-piece
racing suit scandalized a public accustomed
to seeing women dressed in cumbersome swimming dress — two to six alb... introducing them.
new swimming styles were marketed by
Kellerman. Jantzen, and Bocce knitting Mills
started carrying s...
...orted made
in 1910s.

① ② ③ ④ ⑤ ⑥ ⑦ ⑧ ⑨ ⑩

NEDERLAND
JULIANA REGINA
1.50 GULDEN

41Tab-w...
I pray...
that your
is bles...
good w...
| day | |

No.12-mosp...
The ticket of the ship

57843

— Potentill...

Practical
Beauty & Value

Edition
CREATIVITY
...TO-DAY USES
...ND NOTE-TAKING

Preface

The moment I heard the news that Lin Deng was about to write this book, my heart leaped. Finally, I thought, her journaling secrets will be revealed.

I remember the first time I saw Lin Deng's journals on line; I couldn't stop looking at them over and over again, thinking how this journaling artist was doing something that went away beyond writing things down. It bothered me that, compared to her artistic expression, my own stereotypical thinking about what a journal should look like had kept me recording life on dull pages of words. I quickly gathered some materials and followed suit, but I have to confess that while Lin Deng's journal appeared so richly focused, mine seemed piteously disordered. Strangely enough though, my first attempt didn't upset me or feel like a failure. On the contrary, it gave me a wonderful glow of satisfaction.

The half hour I spent sticking pieces together randomly on the pages remained vivid in my memory—a valuable time of working peacefully by myself. Later, I began to question whether a journal could be made with text only, and wondered what had made me so happy about my first pictorial journal, despite its faults.

I share the opinion with most people that, from a distance, keeping a journal is a kind of lifestyle habit. But from a closer point of view, it is a very private hobby. Like others who journal, I might sometimes want to record my thoughts after eating a delicious piece of cake, but I also hope to express my joy and sadness, share and record my inner feelings and give full vent to my emotions, which no one else needs to know about. And, in addition, I'm always looking for ways to enjoy solitude other than browsing through microblogs on my cellphone or watching dramas on my iPad.

I completely indulged in the 30-minute process of combining different materials on paper, thoroughly enjoying myself, free of any self consciousness or limits. The joyous feeling of finishing a collage has not faded since I started. I don't worry about recording anything in writing during the collage process, I prefer it to be a pure and honest form of self expression.

Lin Deng's journaling left a deep impression on me the first time I saw it, so it's no wonder that I was excited by the news that she was publishing her journal secrets, which include details of her working process, collaging methods, and drawing skills.

Now, I am looking forward to putting together another superb journal page and enjoying solitary moments of collaging with the help of tips and tricks from Lin Deng.

Bushimen
Lifestyle microblogger

Author's Preface

How can you enjoy a long life without doing useless things?

—Xiang Hongzuo (1798-1835)

When I started writing this book, there were so many points that I wanted to cover: who I am, how I got into journaling, why I decided to write about it, and how I feel about it. I didn't know if I had managed to incorporate all of my thoughts into the book until I reached the end.

Writing

Writing is so much harder than I expected.

Before setting out to write, I looked at a lot of journaling books on the market to find out what sorts of questions needed answering. I also made a note of many of the questions frequently asked on microblogs.

After much deliberation, I decided to put together a book on how to make a distinctive journal for those who are just beginning to indulge in the pastime. The three most important areas that I cover in this book are: collecting materials, designing layouts and matching colors, and recording content. But all of it, from beginning to end, is infused with my thoughts about my journaling life and attitudes.

Materials, layout, colors, and journaling systems are the key words that come up frequently on my microblog, so I systematically organized my journals and analyzed my rules and preferences for using layout and colors and for choosing materials.

This was the first time that I had inspected my work so systematically since becoming interested in journaling three years ago. I tried to sort out the making processes and transform them into words. Thus, this has grown into a sharing experience as well as a means of presenting bits and pieces of knowledge in a systematic way.

As a journaling lover who is not a graduate in design, I prefer to use a straight forward approach in depicting my journaling methods and styles. For instance, the terms I used for layout and color-matching methods may not conform to professional design standards but they are the terms I have found most useful for reference, and that have survived my multiple experiments.

Journaling and my life

I have spent three years exploring journaling and growing fond of it.

Many people have asked me what the point of a journal is, but I usually fail to answer them fluently. I am a journaling hobbyist and love making collages. It is a pleasant process to turn a blank notebook into one that is rich and colorful. Journaling is definitely not a process for improving efficiency—instead it often gobbles up my time.

In my view, journaling is a way to keep records as well as a hobby. Like painting, flower arranging, and tea tasting, it might seem to have no practical use, and yet it provides us with a delightful and fulfilling experience. Every time I open one of my journals, look through the notes and comments that I wrote about myself and my activities at a certaindate in the past, I laugh or find myself missing those good old days.

Of course, journaling is not completely perfect for me—it can get costly. The phrase I use to describe the time I devote to it is: addicted to journaling, short on cash. But this "shortage" has nothing to do with a shortage of soul or spirit.

Life would be unbearable if it were restricted solely to so-called meaningful things. Value in the worldly sense is not what I pursue. How can you enjoy a long life without doing useless things?

Many of my microblog followers have told me that after they begin keeping a journal, they also begin reading, or expressing a desire to practice calligraphy and painting, or to work on managing their time better, or to work out regularly and follow a healthy diet. They want to change themselves for the better and to lead a rich life. I think those are some of the unexpected and magical powers that journaling gives us.

Lin Deng

Contents

Chapter 1

JOURNALING
AND ME

- **Retro Style—Collecting Moments**
- **My Retro Journal**

Although every element is drawn from a different era or place, the passage of time gives each a retro look.

March

CAFÉ & BRASSERIE
11-15/18-23

März
30
Freitag

Wo 13   Karfreitag   2018

Collection de A. A.
Nr. 1073
(poliert...
Loc. Min...
Franz...
M. 45.- Dr. P. K...
Rheinisches Mine...
Bonn am...

preening... in all honesty, I was surprised to find how
long months of traveling, of retreat and battle with
d been reduced to my basic essence, ...ival and
would have been entirely irrelevant, even had I
expected to find...

Section 01

RETRO STYLE
—COLLECTING MOMENTS

They say that those born under the sign of Cancer are stay-at-home oldies freaks. As a typical Cancerian, I'm obsessed with everything vintage and have a great curiosity and awe for all old things.

Retro style is infused with a sense of age; it might recall something that was popular in the past or revive a trend after it is out of date. The style originates with nostalgia. Someone once said that nostalgia is the pain of an old wound, a twinge in your heart, and far more powerful than memory alone.

Lining up patterned tapes on a page

My Favorite Retro Styles

In my eyes, retro style means

Symmetrical Victorian layout designs, elaborate and refined typefaces and patterns;

The ethereal, intertwining plant patterns of William Morris's world;

The Seasons series and Slav Epic in the Art Nouveau designs of Alphonse Mucha;

Delicate watercolors of flowers created by Pierre-Joseph Redouté;

Modern women in Hollywood's golden age;

Chinese scroll painting and peonies;

Elegant, graceful Audrey Hepburn;

Enchanting seas of flowers in Polaroid pictures;

...

All of these deeply touch the retro center in my soul.

I am attracted to a retro style that revives lost youth by setting it in a notebook, keeping it in a journal, and locking it in my mind. In my journal collages, these retro elements reflect my enthusiasm and even my desire to catch moments in history and the richness of years.

There are thousands of retro styles and elements. The eight styles I like most are shown on the following pages.

I often use these elements in my collages. Although they come from different times, and different regions, they all lend a similar sense of nostalgia and speak to me.

// The gorgeous, complex, and symmetrical patterns of the Victorian Age

// The intertwining plants used as decorative patterns in William Morris's creations

// The lifelike and vivid flower illustrations drawn by Pierre-Joseph Redouté

// The beauties in The Seasons painted by Alphonse Maria Mucha, a leader of the Art Nouveau movement

// The most eye-catching modern women in Hollywood's golden age

// Delicate Chinese peony and bird paintings

// Eternally elegant and beautiful Audrey Hepburn in pictures

// Pictures of beautiful girls and seas of flowers taken with Polaroid camera in the 1980s

Section 02

MY RETRO JOURNAL

There are all kinds of touching trifles in our lives that we want to remember. Journaling is like a piece of amber preserving an insect from the past. I don't expect that I'll be able to recall all of the minutiae when I read my journals fused with these retro elements in my old age, but writing my memories in the present puts me in a good mood.

I want to record something about my life, and I prefer to do it in an engaging way. That's why I stay passionate about journaling.

"Journaling is like preserving life in amber," is what I wrote in November 2016 when I finished by the first traveler's notebook.

The Characteristics of My Retro Journal

• Full page: I get used to filling a whole page in my retro journal.

• Multiple layers and various materials: I have a habit of collecting all kinds of paper things which will be used to overlie and glue materials together in collage.

• Retro colors: I prefer retro colors such as brown, dark red and dark green which make my journal in an old style.

• Plant elements: Almost all of my journaling have plant elements.

• Emphasis on layout: Usually I consider the layout and main colors first and then choose material to glue.

The Simple Process of Journaling

Tools: 1. Tapes 2. Seals 3. Inkpad 4. Date stamp 5. Glue dots 6. Printed material 7. Notebook 8. Scissors

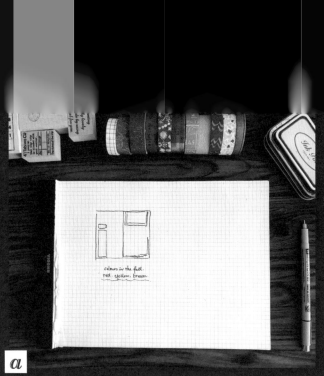
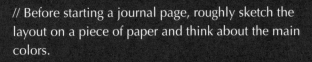

a

// Before starting a journal page, roughly sketch the layout on a piece of paper and think about the main colors.

// For example, I wanted to create the feeling of maple leaves turning red, so I chose red, yellow and brown as the main colors.

b

// Using the main colors as a base, select the appropriate tapes and materials in the same tone.

c

// Refer to the layout draft to finish the largest section of the page. Use a bunch of roses as the floral motif with a retro yellowish cutout pattern as the background. Overlap and glue them to the lower-left corner.

d

// Glue the same background pattern to the upper-right corner to correspond. Add details to the lower-left section to enrich the layers. Glue on a reddish-brown strip to underscore the section.

// I finished the three decorated parts of the layout: The lower left corner has the main decoration, the upper and lower right have small decorations. I added more layers and details to these sections individually.

//Add the journaling date to the blank space, then adjust the details of different layers to make the arrangement more balanced. All decorated parts are completed and the next step is to write.

// It's best to keep the writing consistent with the colors you've chosen so that the layout will be clean and neat. Decide on the word space according to the length of the content.

// In writing, you can also try different text directions and typefaces to add variety.

// Use a different paragraph for each subject. That will help you find them easily, and it looks enchanting.

// The pages are complete.

// In photographing these pages, I added some interesting leaves and berries, a ribbon poking out from underneath and a glimpse of some of the tapes I like to use.

// These are my usual steps for making a retro journal. Isn't it simple?

Pictures of Details

NOTE: You can download many collage materials from the Internet. The content I used are examples, but you can use or write whatever you want in your journaling.

All sorts of bits of life that normally float away from us can be glued into a notebook and retained as memories.

Chapter 2

JOURNAL MAKING

- Collecting Materials
- Designing Layouts and Collage
- Matching Colors
- Recording
- Improving Journaling

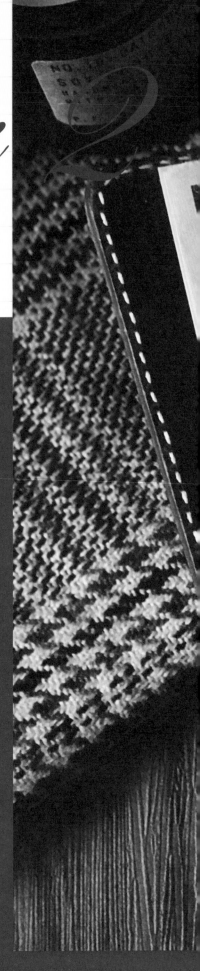

COLLECTING MATERIALS

My Frequently Used Materials

I think many people are confused by two journaling questions: what materials to look for, and what materials are the most appropriate? Because I have a strong preference for certain retro elements, they show up in my journals with high frequency. Here I will share nine of my favorites with you.

01
Basic Types of Tapes

I would find it very hard to do journaling without tapes, so I have collected many basic and sold-colored varieties that are subtle, practical, and that often help to decide the tone and color of a page.

// The dark brown tape strips not only divide the page into sections, but also connect and unify the upper-left and lower-right corners.

// The two red tape strips emphasize the dominant color of the page and brighten it.

// The brown tape strips contrast sharply with the green leaves, enhancing the visual impact.

// Green tape, one of my favorites, coordinates with plant elements with its patterns and color.

02

Stamps for Improving Details

Stamps can improve a layout so I have collected many retro stamps for text, numbers, receipts, and flowers.

// A large area of text below the main element is stamped with a seal and claret-red ink.

// The red title stamping blends with and overlaps part of the khaki sunflower seal, showing off the richness of layers.

// In the upper-right corner, a receipt seal stamped in deep blue is underscored with a line of light brown, creating an attractive secondary area of decoration.

// The numbers 10 and 30 are stamped. Number stamps are very useful in journaling.

03

Plants and Large Flowers

Flowering plants are among the most common elements in my retro collages. Because of my love for flowers and plants I'm forever cutting them out and gluing them into place, matching them with other materials. They inspire me a lot.

// The black-and-white flower covering the retro strip is eye-catching and harmonious within the layout.

// The branch of white flowers under the image of the girl freshens the entire page.

// The bright yellow flower set off by strips of brown tape determines the predominant color of the layout.

// The red and white flowers repeat the colors found in the retro-patterned strips of tape. The layout is enlivened by a girl on a swing.

04

Girls from Different Eras

I love using plants and flowers in my collages and like to match the flowers with pretty girls. The girls have their own style and come from different eras and become even more attractive when paired with plants in my journal.

// The silhouette of the dancing ballerina is glued over two basic tape strips.

// The girl wearing a classical tutu is glued on top of blue flowers.

// A girl gathers up her skirts and walks toward

// The girl holding a red rose is inserted among the patterns

05

Retro Intertwining Plant Patterns

Because of fascination with William Morris's designs, I fall hopelessly in love with all retro intertwining plant patterns. Medieval plant patterns are also very useful background elements in collages.

// The blue and white flowers together with the deep blues and golden browns convey a strong nostalgic flavor.

// Green and yellow colors belong to the tropical rain forest. Patterns with a strong jungle sense show off these bright colors.

// The golden bloom of the fireworks against the sapphire background is dazzling, but also orderly.

// Gold and orange plant patterns intertwining with floral stems are mysterious and exotic.

06

Newspaper, Old Books, and Printed Text

Along with the content that I write in my journal, I like to add other textual elements in collage. These work very well with pictures, giving a page a dynamic look.

// The simple and straightforward technique of using newspaper as a background creates a wonderfully nostalgic look. Newspaper is a natural background material.

// Here I expanded the area of the text so that the girl appears to be dancing over the words.

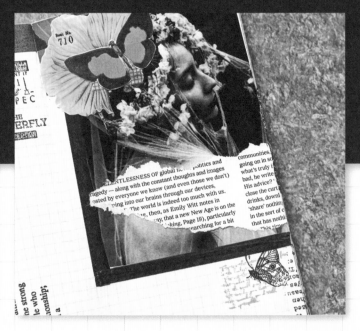

// The page is composed of magazine text and other colorful pieces. They are well-arranged and harmonious.

// Irregular, hand-torn fragments of magazine text are glued into place. They help to break up the original version's structure, making it vivid but not rigid.

07

Retro Numbers and Stickers

Numbers and stickers are multi-purpose materials in my collages because they decorate the page, coordinate with the content, and sometimes serve as a date or page number.

// The combination of stickers and numbers enriches the layers without looking messy.

// I chose large numerals for this collage. They add an eye-catching emphasis, highlighted by the red frame.

// Applying an opaque sticky label that is white and black, breaks the usual rules of design and enriches the layout.

// The large numbers with their black and white retro coloring correspond with the background and enliven the subdued colors.

08

Images of Scenery with a Cinematic Effect

I have collected many images of scenery in the style of Polaroid photos; most of them include flowers. I love the bright colors. Whether they are solo on a page or combined with other elements in a collage, they can have a striking effect.

// The bright red flowers against the turquoise sky are eye-catching and compelling even without any extra elements.

// I love pictures of girls picking flowers in a whole sea of flowers so I let this one occupy half a page.

// Partially covered by the photo of the girl and orange flowers, the big purple iris sets a warm and cozy mood.

// This whole page is highlighted with bright yellow and green colors. The sunflowers in bloom instantly create a happy mood that lasts all day.

09

Retro Tickets and Postage Stamps

Both the stamps sealed on ordinary mail envelopes and colorful tickets are my favorite small collection all the time. They are the representatives of retro objects and show the elapse of time when stuck to a notebook.

// I added an orange-red stamp to the bright background.

// The tiny old ticket that I found adds a strong nostalgic element with its typeface and style.

// The Chinese bird painting and the western plant illustration both have a retro style, and blend with a special, pleasing quality.

// The two retro stamps below the butterfly create a predominate yellow tone.

Collecting materials is an intriguing activity. I enjoy the process of searching for and cutting up these bits of ephemera. As I go about day-to-day life, it's not hard to find all kinds of materials worth saving and gluing into a notebook. A leaf or a ribbon, if they please me, can be invited into my journal as an important guest.

01

Back Issues

The newspapers and magazines you have finished reading are excellent journaling materials. The pictures in newspapers and magazines have very special colors that tapes and stickers do not share. Making full use of them can create your own journaling style and save costs.

Virtually every variety of magazine can be cut and used as you want. I often search for materials from fashion, home and travel magazines, Japanese magazines and English newspapers.

A.
Fashion Magazines

Many of my magazine materials come from fashion magazines, where the great variety of stylish girls and their clothes make useful collage materials.

Characteristics of fashion magazine photos include: rich colors, diverse textures, and distinctive patterns matched with clothes. These combinations can be more harmonious than the ones we come up with ourselves and can be used directly as journal-page backgrounds.

// The skirt of the model on the right is used as a background. The girl in the picture below it comes from the same magazine.

// The model on the left is cut from a magazine and used as the main focus of the layout.

B.
Travel Magazines

Characteristics of travel magazine photos include: exotic images and colors from nature. Photographs of scenery from travel magazines can be gorgeous and colorful, and they are among my favorite sources for journal-page backgrounds.

// The sunset's glow, bright blue of the sea, and beige cliffs add color to the page that the tapes and sticker don't provide.

// I cut a picture of exotic, colorful houses into pieces and combined them

C.
Home Magazines

Characteristics of travel magazines include: solid wood colors, wallpapers of different patterns, and house decorations of all kinds. These can be mixed freely in a journal. The wood-toned photos that appear in home magazines are a good choice if you want to use dark colors or shades of green as a background or on a large page.

// This green pattern is cut from a picture of wallpaper in a magazine.

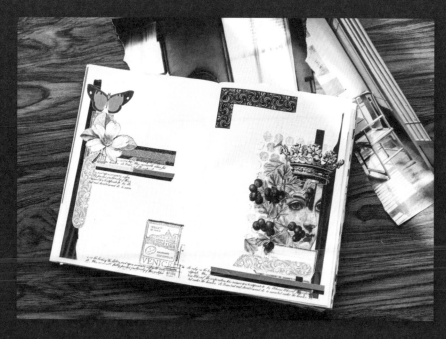

// This page border is cut from a picture of solid wood furniture in a home magazine.

D.
Japanese Magazines

Characteristics of Japanese magazines include: pictures that are neatly arranged so that they can be cut easily, and pictures that are fresh in style and that focus on scenes from life. The paper used in Japanese magazines is not overly reflective and blends with other paper elements.

// The four green pictures all come from the magazine, *One Day*.

// The two pictures of the tea plantation on the right are cut from the magazine, *Hiyori Techo*.

E.

English Newspapers

Characteristics of English newspapers include: a sense of nostalgia evoked by the texture of the paper, typefaces, and layouts. The color of the paper fits in well anywhere. English newspaper can serve as the background in many layouts.

// I tore the newspaper corner by hand and glued it on the top of other materials.

// Newspaper forms the background of the right-hand page.

02

Greeting Cards and Postcards

I save the birthday cards, invitations, and postcards that I buy when I travel or receive from my friends in a little box. The most meaningful ones will be glued to the pages of my journal, like the postcards shown in the insert and the added page, below. In this way, In this way, they add their own character to the book.

// I like to buy local postcards when I travel to cities, and glue them in my notebook.

// This postcard records a street scene in old Beijing. A journaling friend sent it to me.

// Sometimes magazines and books contain free postcards. I pick my favorites and keep them in my notebook.

// I glued a postcard from a friend into my notebook to keep a record of that day.

03
Receipts, Maps, and Pamphlets in Daily Life

Publicity cards, maps, and flight tickets are part of my usual collections and are definitely useful materials in journaling collage. They bear witness to my life when I paste them on the pages, enriching the layout leaving a record of life for my memories.

// This is the receipt for souvenirs that I bought on a trip.

// This is a pamphlet of tourist attraction that I visited.

// This is a hotel map a receptionist gave me when I was checking in.

// This is a local map that I collected on my trip. After trimming off the edge, I added it to my notebook.

04

The Materials Easily Ignored in Daily Life

Ever since I started keeping a journal, I have collected bits and pieces of things that I come across, such as stunning hotel cards, and the packaging that comes with online shopping. When you observe them carefully, you're observing life. Beautiful materials are everywhere.

A.

Dried Flowers and Fallen Leaves

Dried flowers and fallen leaves can be natural ornaments in a notebook. They reflect my habit of picking up all sorts of leaves and flowers along the road in spring and autumn. As they fade, carefully pluck the petals from a rose and place them between sheets of paper until they dry. Once they are dried, flowers can be glued to journal pages.

// The first time I drew roses, I cut leaves from a bush to decorate them. I flattened and dried the leaves in a thick book and then added them to the notebook.

All Kinds of Paper Products

Believe it or not, wrap-around book bands, instructions that come with cosmetics, wine labels, and flower wrappers all find their way into my collages.

// On the left page, the floral background was cut from the instructions that came with an English cosmetic.

// The yellow English paper applied to the journal page adds a retro style.

// The big flower, cut from wrapping paper, is overlapped with a girl on a swing to make the page

// I peeled this wine label off a bottle and glued it into my notebook. I like its pattern and color

Along with all sorts of wrapping paper, I collect a variety of printing papers and explore different printing effects. There are at least forty kinds of printing paper to experiment with, and many printing techniques on paper that are suitable for collage.

01

The Choice of Printer

I have tried three types of printers: color inkjet printers, color laser printers, and Polaroid instant photo printers. Here is what I discovered.

	Machine Price (Unit: USD)	Printing Definition	Printing Pages (with one change of ink box, selenium drum and photo paper)	Printing Speed	Color Deviation	Consumable Accessories	Machine Maintenance
Color Inkjet Printer	44–74	Clear	200–300 pages	quick	A little bit	Ink box and ink jet	Need to use it frequently to prevent ink box from drying out
Color Laser Printer	More than 148	Clear	2000 pages	Very quick	Very little	Selenium drum	None
Polaroid Instant Photoprinter	192–222	Not very clear	10 pieces of paper as a set	A little slow	Some	Photo paper	None

Color Inkjet Printer

Advantage: Color inkjet printer, including its accessories, are cheaper than other printers so the total of printing cost is low. Printed images are sharp and clear except for a little bit color deviation.

Disadvantage: The ink box has to be changed often and the color inkjet printer is slower than a laser printer. You need to use it frequently to prevent the ink box from drying out.

Applicable User: Newcomers who do not require high color accuracy and who do not need to print a great number of materials quickly

Color Laser Printer

Advantages: It works quickly, pictures are clear with little color deviation and its selenium drum can be used for a long time.

Disadvantage: It has a low price performance ratio. The printer and its accessories are expensive.

Applicable User: Anyone who needs to print a large amount of materials

Polaroid Instant Photoprinter

Advantages: The printer is small and portable. You can print at any time you want when traveling. Polaroid instant photos can be used directly in journaling.

Disadvantages: The Polaroid photo paper is a little expensive and the photos are not very clear, so it is not suitable for printing important materials.

Applicable User: Anyone who loves traveling and printing pictures daily

A.

Three Types of Printers and Their Printing Examples

// The original printed materials (electronic version)

// Pictures printed with a Polaroid instant photoprinter

// Pictures with the same content printed with three types of printer

From left to right: color inkjet printer, color laser printer, and Polaroid instant photoprinter

// The same printing paper used in a laser printer (left) and inkjet printer (right)

// The color of the picture printed with an inkjet printer (right) is very different from the original, while the color from the laser printer (left) is closer.

B.

Collages with the Printed Materials

// Inkjet printer (left) and laser printer (right)

// Inkjet printer (left) and laser printer (right)

Printing Effects of Different Types of Paper

Paper products are the most important materials in journaling collages. Tapes, stickers, sticky notes, receipts, pamphlets, and greeting cards are some of my favorite materials that I use in my notebooks. Different types of paper have different textures. Choosing the appropriate paper products for the multiple layers of a collage is a crucially important step.

A.
Common Paper

The paper that I use most often includes writing paper, kraft paper, and tracing paper. Along with these, I have collected a variety of colorful papers. If interested, you also experiment with printing on art paper, such as rag, photographique, embossed pinstripe paper, and Arches aquarelle.

Kraft Paper

Kraft paper is great for creating nostalgic elements, so I often use it for printing.

There are kraft paper of various weights and colors on the market. Take care to identify the weight and color when you shop.

I usually buy 70-80g light color kraft paper. Deep color may affect the printing results and paper that is too heavy will shorten the life of the printer and make the notebook bulky.

I like crafting with kraft paper, such as making bookmarks. Sometimes I draw on them.

The price of kraft paper is very reasonable. You can buy a package of 100 sheets for only about $1.50.

// The butterfly is printed on kraft paper.

Tracing Paper

Tracing paper is the one of the paper products that appears constantly in my journal. I often print beautiful graphics on tracing paper as a separator page or an inserted page for its qualities of opacity and strength.

The paper's transparency allows light to pass through, lends a sense of layers to a page, and reveals the patterns underneath.

// The white flower is printed on single-layer tracing paper and then glued to the middle of the page.

One of the great advantages of adhesive paper is its convenience. Since it is already sticky, you can simply cut out the patterns and position them directly onto a page. Adhesive paper is suitable for small patterns, such as numbers and letters. You can also store and transport them after printing and cutting the patterns.

Because of the adhesive on the back, this paper is a little thick. Before printing, make sure your printer is compatible with this type of paper, or it could easily get stuck in the machine.

I often use sticky writing paper, sticky kraft paper, and sticky tracing paper, and sometimes sticky washi, sticky synthetic paper, sticky transparent PVC, sticky xuan paper, and sticky textured paper. You can try all of these after confirming they are compatible with your printer.

Sticky writing paper (matte)

Sticky writing paper (glossy)

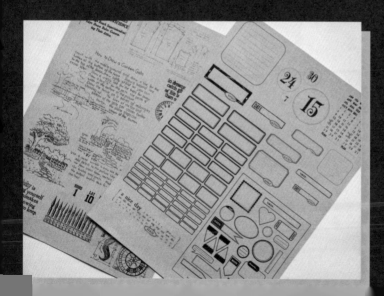

Sticky Washi

Adhesive washi, more often called washi tape, is softer and easier for writing than tracing paper. For the sake of convenience, I like to print the text I plan to use later in collage on washi paper.

// The black and white flower is printed on sticky washi. It is translucent, making the newspaper words partly visible.

Sticky Textured Paper

Printing ink on sticky paper will not be very dense; it allows a clear outline of patterns depending on the roughness of the paper surface. Sticky textured paper is appropriate for use as a the background. I like this product much, because of its attractive yellowish color and special texture which create an extraordinary nostalgic ambiance.

// The leaf is printed on sticky textured paper.

03
Multiple-Purpose Paper

Paper can have a powerful effect, and not just for printing. All sorts of paper products that we collect can present a unique charm in our journals if used properly.

// I tore the light kraft paper roughly by hand, and used it as the background. This technique adds a look of age to a journal page.

// Kraft paper can also be used for wrapping. Wrapped with kraft paper, little gifts for friends can easily be decorated.

// The flower is stamped on paper with a rubber stamp. After it is cut out, it can be applied as a sticker.

// Tracing paper is used as a separator page after printing and stamping the text. Here you can see

Gadgets for Making Materials More Useful

In the process of collecting and cutting materials, I find many interesting and efficient tools. Here I will share them with you.

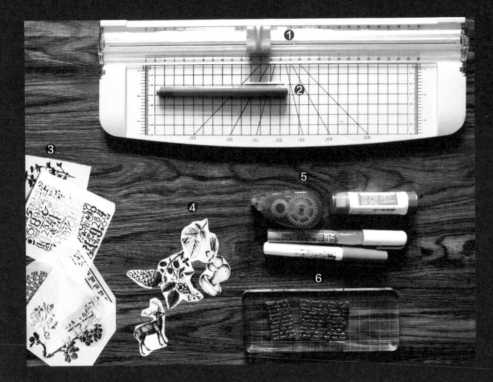

Tools: 1. Paper trimmer
2. Pen cutter
3. Stencil template
4. Release paper
5. Glue
6. Acrylic stamp block

A.

Paper Trimmer

A paper trimmer is helpful in trimming the edges of printed materials such as magazine and newspaper pages neatly. The great advantage of a paper trimmer is in aligning margins and cutting large sheets of paper quickly and conveniently. I often use mine to cut magazine pages into strips like tapes.

B.

Pen Cutter

A pen cutter is a tool that looks like a pen but has a cutting tip instead of a pen point. It is very convenient for use in cutting pictures of plants and people out of magazines without rough edges.

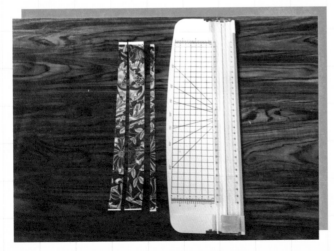

C.

Release Paper

Release paper allows you to cut the clear edges of taped graphics. If you cut the tapes directly, the graphic will easily stick to your hand. Release paper makes the cutting and storing sticky graphics easily.

Books of release paper are available online. These make carrying tapes and stickers easy when you travel, but they are expensive, so you may want to use them sparingly.

D.

All Sorts of Glue

1. Glue dots: These are my favorite glue products. They are convenient to use and keep the surface neat. Their sticky surfaces will not damage paper. Even changing the positions of materials on a page will not cause problems.

2. Pen-shaped glue stick/liquid glue: These are suitable for gluing small areas or small joints and will prevent unwanted excess glue.

3. Square glue stick: the square shape helps in applying glue neatly along the right-angled edge of a piece of paper, glue evenly, and prevent the glue stick from rolling away.

4. Paste: This is suitable for large-area gluing. Paste is highly cost effective and practical.

E.

Acrylic Stamp Block

An acrylic stamp block is an auxiliary tool for a transparent stamp. It guarantees that the stamp will be applied with even pressure on the stamp pad, for an even printed line.

F.

Stencil Template

Based on the theory of positive and negative shapes, when you color and remove a stencil template, the clear lines of pattern will emerge.

Its function is similar to that of stamp, but it can be used with an inkpad, watercolor, colored pencils etc.

Section 02

LAYOUT AND COLLAGE

// I like every well-arranged page of my journal.
As shown here, you can still see its neatness and
attractiveness even when it is soft-focused.

My Layout Methods and Experience

The more time I devote to collaging, the more I find myself wanting to create pages that are both specific in style, and pleasing to the eye. After some careful research into layout design, I summarized some important principles and I will share them here with you.

I am accustomed to looking at the left and the right pages as a whole. If the spread is to be filled with a day's worth of contents, it must have a unified layout. The following examples all demonstrated the layouts of full spreads.

Usually, I start by dividing a page into the main element area, secondary element area, and text area.

Main Element Area, Secondary Element Area, and Text Area

1. The main element area is the largest and in the most prominent position. It is usually completed first.

2. The secondary element responds to the main element, serves as its supplement, and enriches the layout.

3. The text area is where we write down our words. It is usually the final step.

According to the number of main elements, the layout designs fall into three types.

01

Only One Main Element

When there is only one main element on the page, it becomes a focus and its colors create the whole atmosphere. The position of the main element determines the layout of the others.

According to the position of the main element, the layout patterns fall into four types—center-margin, top-bottom, left-right, and encircling structure.

A.

Center-Margin

The main element is placed in the middle of page to achieve a symmetry that evokes order and neatness. It is also one of the most fundamental and easy layout designs to help beginners get started.

// The bunch of white flowers and the dancing girl are the main elements. The tape strips and stamps around them are the secondary elements. The picture is placed in the middle of the spread while the text is put on both sides of the main and secondary elements.

// Here the main element is half with a flower background picture and half with a smiling face. The sticker and stamp in the upper left corner are secondary elements. The content is in the center of the spread and text on both sides of the main elements.

// The main elements here are composed of a ballerina, retro patterns, and butterfly. The stamp on the right is a secondary element. I mixed various images and materials to compose the main element.

// The main elements here are composed of two pictures: a butterfly and a seal. On this page I do not use any secondary element. The text surrounding the main elements gives a pleasing composition to the design.

B.
Top-Bottom

The main element and text divide the page into top and bottom sections. This composition provides a solid, neat, and interesting basis for a layout design. A flexible approach to the positioning of the text and secondary element will create a vivid layout. This is an easy layout design for newcomers. You can also try it with unequal sections above and below.

// The main element is located below while the text is placed in the center and top. It creates balance, harmony, and visual stability.

// The text area is located under the main elements. A medium yellow tape strip divides the page into the main element and text section. All of the elements come together to form one cohesive design.

// I sometimes find it visually interesting when I write horizontally by turning the notebook. The main and secondary elements divide the page into two, while the text section leaves room for two days' feelings. Information blocks create a rich and sharp layout.

// There are four days' feelings recorded in the text section with a picture as the main element. The layout of the top and bottom is simple but not monotonous here.

C.
Left-Right

The layout is divided into left and right sections by the main element, and responds to the text section. The left-right format is my most frequently used layout. Its focus gives flexibility and unity to a composition. The main element anchors and stabilizes it, and the various shapes of the white spaces increase the breathing space within the borders. It's important to keep the left and right borders in mind when you are arranging elements.

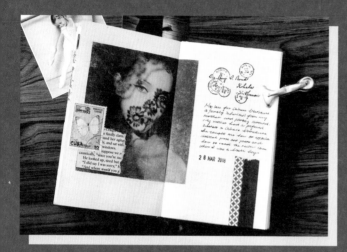

// The main element is positioned to the left and stretched over the central axis. White space is left in the upper and lower margins. The text and secondary elements are treated as a unit. The whole layout is divided into the left and right parts.

// This is the most basic left-right structure. The girl with a flower on her head is the main element, the text section fills the center, and the secondary element appears to the right. This arrangement is visually balanced, uniform, and elegant.

// The left-right layout is also suitable for a large area of white space. The flower of the main element doesn't take over the whole left page, but the white space and them flower are regarded as one and the same is true for the text and secondary element to the right. In this way, the layout creates breathing space and stays neat and organized.

// I used tape to decorate the central axis and set up the left-right structure. The roses occupy one whole page of the spread, matched with some secondary elements. There is more white space to the right to enhance the breathing room.

D.
Encircling

A layout where the main element encircles the text or the text encircles the main element can be called an encircling structure. It is usually used to fully cover a spread. I often employ this arrangement to the passport-size Traveler's Notebook (TN) or A6 notebook for maximum writing and decorating. But under this layout, you should choose only one object of reference to encircle or the layout may lose focus and appear messy.

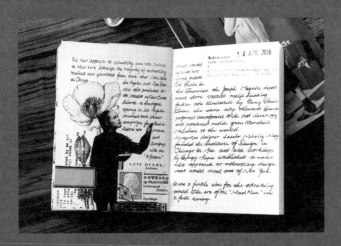

// The format of text encircling elements can be applied to the design when there is a lot of writing on the page. Avoid too many scrappy elements that will make the layout appear disordered.

// A layout encircled with lines makes a neat, clear frame.

// This design also uses lines and main elements to frame the text. The tape serves the function of separating and highlighting.

// I applied both encircling and left-right structures here. The combination of layout methods can enrich the layers of design and show diversity.

02
Two Main-Element Areas

To add more collage elements to the page and avoid monotony, sometimes I put two main elements on the same page. And these can be two collage types: elements in the same size and elements in different sizes. They can also be used combined with the above-mentioned four layout designs.

A.
Elements in the Same Size

// When I say elements of the same size, it doesn't mean that they completely equal in area. Instead, it means they have similar sizes. I prefer to arrange materials diagonally and leave some white space to create breathing space.

// This layout has a left-right structure with some white space on the top and bottom. The positions of the two main elements encircle the text area from the left and the right. In layout design, you can employ one or two methods to enrich the page but remember not to use more than two methods. Otherwise it become disordered.

// On the left page, a large main element and secondary element occupy the largest area, while the text section is small. On the right page, the main and secondary elements have a simple design and some white space. The whole layout achieves a sense of balance without constraints.

// The large letters are the main elements here and placed in a prominent position. Don't be afraid of making the letters too large or too small. What's important is to place them in the right position where they will provide the finishing touch.

B.
Elements in Different Sizes

// The blue peony and girl dressed in brownish red are two main elements. To avoid disorder, I employed a diagonal arrangement which is the tidiest way to arrange elements. The text section allows flexibility and white space. You don't need to fill every corner of a page.

// Sometimes it is hard to distinguish between a small main element and a secondary element. Don't worry about that, just follow the principle of secondary elements: Two small pictures can serve the roles of both main and secondary elements at the same time.

// Sometimes a secondary element can become a focus of a page. In this example, the red tape strip running through the page divides the spread into left-right parts that form a whole.

// The white space is regarded as an element here. After gluing in a piece of kraft paper to the left, the blank space can be viewed as a white tape strip, part of the main element. Compared with the right, it becomes a larger main element.

03

No Main Element Area

If the notebook is too small or we don't want to have our records decorated too much, several stickers, tape strips, or stamps are good enough to beautify the page. I call it as a no-main-element principle.

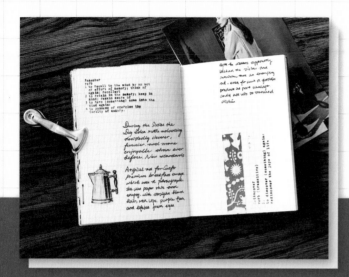

// My most frequently used notebook is a TN notebook of passport size. Due to its small size, a page can contain only few words and decorations.

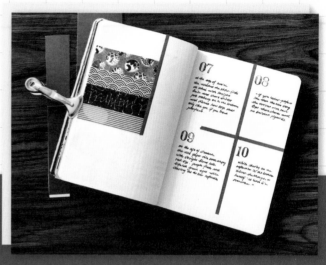

// If I want a simple layout, I will often divide the page into two parts, one for collage and the other for records. It is convenient when you are looking for something that you had written earlier.

// Without a main material, I often decorate the page with tape strips. In this composition, the top and bottom sections are very useful. The two tape strips create the text area, framing and adorning the contents.

// No main element design is good for clarifying records, so I choose tapes with plain and simple patterns. They have light colors to make the page clean and elegant.

Different Layouts for Different Sizes of Notebook

The size of a notebook determines its function. For example, I choose the small and thin Traveler's Notebook (hereafter referred to as TN) of passport size as my portable schedule when I go out. When I record trifles or feelings I prefer a bigger A5 squared notebook. When I need to do journaling for travel, I use the TN of standard size.

As far as I am concerned, since different sizes of notebooks have different amounts of content, they need corresponding types of layout.

I'll show you a number of different layouts that I use on different sizes of notebooks.

1 TN of passport size

2 A6 dot matrix notebook (Fabriano)

3 B6 slim notebook (Midori, hereafter referred to as MD)

4 TN of standard size

5 A5 lined notebook (Moleskine)

01

A5 Notebook

Size: 148mm*210mm

An A5 notebook has large areas for writing, so it can be used as a jottings notebook, a reading journal, a movie journal, or an inspiration journal.

// I often make a large collage when writing my daily thoughts in an A5 notebook. If I have a lot to say, the collage will be smaller and vice versa.

// Adding simple collages can make the pages elegant and tidy if an A5 notebook is merely used for keeping schedules.

// If there are few words on a page, a large area of white space in an A5 notebook can create a strong visual impact, especially when opposite a full-page collage. It's easy to create an exciting effect in an A5 notebook. And remember, there is no need to stuff the page no matter how large it is.

// If I don't have much to write and don't intend to leave a lot of white space, I will boldly make collages and encircle the text with main elements.

02

A6 Notebook

Size: 105mm*148mm (half of A5 size)

An A6 notebook is small and can be used as a jotting notebook or a schedule journal when you go out.

// You can easily leave white space in your layouts in an A6 notebook. It won't be as dramatic as in an A5 notebook, but an A6 layout can be harmonious and understated.

// An A6 notebook is perfect for anyone who likes to fill pages with writing. It's easy to do in a notebook this size—in an A5 notebook you would need to combine all the writing with larger collages.

// All sorts of layouts can be composed in an A6 notebook. Here the two main elements are separated left and right to easily accommodate two days' content.

// In this spread there is full page picture on the left and four days' content on the right. This is a good layout in an A6 notebook when I don't have too much to write, but still want to achieve a full-page effect.

03
TN of Standard Size

Size: 110mm*210mm (a bit narrower than an A5 notebook)

A TN of standard size is one of moderate thickness and size and is neither too large nor too small. It can be used as a travel journal, bullet journal, weekly journal or a notebook with gatefolds, inserts, fold-outs, or glued-in pockets for holding small materials.

// Pictures, postcards and receipts can be glued to the travel journal. There are not many pages, so a single notebook is good for one destination. The page size accommodates all sorts of elements, making it easy to experiment. I usually save the materials in the notebook and then design the layout later. Not a tidy process, perhaps, but inspiring!

// These are my TNs for a weekly journal and daily journal.

// A TN of standard size can make use of the simplest left-right layout, or accommodate an added page as a trifold.

// Here are a weekly journal and a daily journal that have the same color tone. The right-hand page holds the main elements and the left is used for content. The daily journal has a little bit of white space while the weekly journal is cramped.

04
TN of Passport Size

Size: 89mm*124mm

A TN of passport is small and can be used as a note journal or an inspiration journal.

// As shown, I use TNs of passport size as my schedule journal with to-do lists and dates, and as an inspiration journal for collecting ideas and images.

// Despite its small size, a passport TN can have room for white space without any other secondary elements.

// When I fail to find any inspiration for color matching, I experiment in a passport size TN. Since it is very small, I can quickly finish collages. And If I hit on any beautiful color matching, I will use it in a big notebook.

// Sometimes I don't want to write, I just want to make collages. Then I take the TN of this size and write down "Nothing has happened today. Good night." Straight up.

05
B6 Slim Notebook (MD)

Size: 105mm*175mm

A MD B6 notebook is slim and makes design easy. It is suitable for any layout, with beautiful white space. A MD B6 notebook is one of moderate thickness, and can be used as an extracts journal, reading journal, jottings journal or travel journal.

// When an MD B6 slim notebook is not filled with full-page elements, it will allow for large or small amounts of white space. Because its length-width ratio is 2:1, a spread is more-or-less square, and allows for a unified and tightly connected layout.

// Filling a page of an MD B6 slim notebook gives you a sense of achievement.

// If you want to try an asymmetrical layout in an MD B6 slim notebook, notebook, place the main elements in the center, and start the text at the upper right. An asymmetric design can be used to good effect, and is easy to achieve in a square format.

// This MD B6 slim notebook makes use of the most common left-right design structure: a main element, a secondary element, and a text area, plus a balance of blank space create a well-composed design.

How to Start

Like me, many journalers buy lots of tapes, stickers, and other elements, but it's not always clear what to do with all of them when you open a blank notebook. In this section we'll cover two methods for getting a clear sense of direction when you don't know what to do.

01

Choose the Main Element and Then the Dominant Color

Looking at the blank pages, think about the images you'd like to see there. Should it be some interesting photos that you took that day, some exquisite restaurant cards, beautiful flower pictures, or maybe a ticket or receipts. First choose the elements, then decide on the dominant hue, based on the colors of the elements.

Element: photographs that I took of autumn leaves in Beijing

Hue: yellow and green

// First I chose the pictures for a collage and roughly identify their colors as yellow and green. The dominant hues of the whole page are deep yellow and deep green so I selected the tone-on-tone tapes and inkpads.

// After figuring out a potential layout, I glued the main elements to the page.

// After deciding on the position of the flowers, I finished the secondary elements of the collage. Then I added some small decorations to unify the two areas.

// I completed this spread of my journal with writing.

Element: a picture of a beautiful girl downloaded and printed from the Internet

Hue: yellow and blue

// Based on the dominant hues of the picture, I selected the tone-on-tone tapes and other secondary elements.

// After working out the layout, I fixed the position of the main elements and decorated them evenly.

// I decided on the position of the secondary elements and added decorations at the same time.

// I chose a tone-on-tone blue pen for writing the content.

02

Choose the Dominant Color and Then the Main Element

If you don't have special images that you want to start with on a blank page, then start with the dominant color for the page, and follow up by finding the elements to go with it.

Hue: red

// Based on the dominant hue, I selected the tone-on-tone elements, tapes, and inkpads.

// After selecting my favorite elements, I determined their positions and decorated them accordingly.

// After I decided on the positions of the secondary elements, I added small decorations at the same time to unify the areas.

// The spread is completed with a balance of writing and white space.

Techniques for Keeping the Layout Tidy and Clean

Many beginners tend to glue all sorts of elements onto a notebook page, which can get messy.

Sometimes it seems as though a mix of elements and a neat layout can't exist in the same space, but in fact they do.

While you work out your collage layouts, pay attention to alignment, white space, and lines, all of which will help to keep your page tidy and clean looking.

Don't do this

The layout fails to have a focus because no thought was given to alignment, blank space, and lines. Also, the border between the main element and secondary element is blurred, causing the visual distraction.

Alignment

Aligned layouts seem to have an invisible line that connects different parts of a page and clarifies them virtually.

In journaling, these can be divided as alignment of text and alignment of pictorial areas.

// The alignment of text on these pages is flush right and flush left. Keeping the text in rectangular blocks helps to create visual order.

// This alignment of text makes the page fresh and legible.

// An alignment of pictorial areas means the elements are arranged in a specific order, as if being framed by an invisible line.

// This page applies alignment of text and alignment of pictorial elements. It is balanced and neat.

02

White Space

Leaving white space is the most effective way of achieving a clean layout. Proper use of white space can create breathing room and prevent the layout from becoming cramped: the principle of "less is more" is displayed perfectly. Sometimes, bold white space can produce a stunning effect.

// In the main element on the left page, white space around the central collage prioritizes the focal point and creates breathing space.

// The tiny spaces between elements are of primary importance. They not only divide the page into sections, but also balance the layout.

// Centering the text and aligning it to the right, has a sophisticated look. Even if the writing is not extensive, this type of composition will not appear unfinished.

// Proper use of white space on the bottom of the page moves the focus upward. Proper use of white space around the text on the left page helps to keep the layout airy.

03
Lines

Framing every area with lines is also a means for a clean layout. Lines can be tapes, strips or drawn by hand.

// I used the narrow tape strips to frame the right half of the text section to improve the layout and highlight the area of text. The lines direct attention to the content.

// The text is also framed with tape strips. The shape of the fame is similar to the rectangle of the main element image, enabling the page to stand out.

// Here, pen lines frame different blocks instead of tape strips. They make the text neat and easy to follow.

// Here, the blocks are also framed by pen lines. Compared with tape strips, they are thin, not obvious, easy to handle, and not distracting.

04

Combination of Alignment, White Space, and Lines

Alignment, white space, and lines can be combined arbitrarily. To some extent, white space and alignment can be regarded as an invisible line. Drawn or taped lines create a visible structure for framing and separating areas, and for making content legible and elegant.

// White space, alignment, and line appear on the page at the same time.

// White space, alignment, and line also appear here at the same time.

// Alignment and white space form the combination used here. They are also my favorite combination.

// I used alignment and white space on this page.

Multi-Layered Collage of Various Elements

I like it when elements overlap and crisscross with each other and only small parts of them can be seen. Usually, I will select their best parts to expose.

Here is something I've learned by instinct: When I write the wrong words or use the wrong elements and can't fix them, I cover my mistakes with collage. I do the same thing when some pictorial element fails to fit into the layout.

Gradually, I find this can lead to a beautiful collage work with rich layers.

01

Start with the Background

The background is the lowest layer of the page and can be chosen from any elements. Sometimes it covers a large area as the secondary element, setting off the main element. Sometimes it can be used as the main element with decorative collaging added around it.

NOTE:

· Different layers should cover and connect with each other.

· When a background serves as the main element, it shouldn't be covered too much or decorated with too many elements.

· Choosing and overlapping elements with different textures will enrich the space and layers.

· Keep harmony among colors.

// The dark red floral background is a secondary element that is used to set off the image of the girl and to establish the tone of the page.

// The picture of two girls is the background as well as the main element, decorated with strips, words, and patterns.

A.

My Most-Used Background Elements

// The elegant flowers serve as the background.

// A ticket stub or receipt can also be used as the background.

// A beautiful picture serves as the background.

// The stamped patterns can be used as the background.

B.
Collage with the Background as Main Element

a

// I chose a picture as the background.

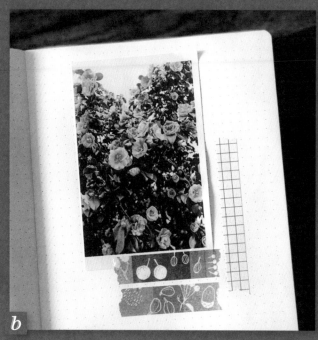

b

// I selected tape strips that share a similar tone with the picture, and glued them around the background.

c

// The tone-on-tone flower and date seals are stamped on the strips to add layers. Oil-based ink is the best choice for the stamp here.

d

// Add more details: English text and yellow tape strips can cover the main element well and build overlapping layers.

C.
Collage with the Background as Secondary Element

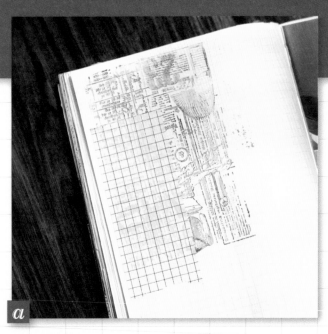

a

// I stamped the page first, then added a plaid strip to break up the design.

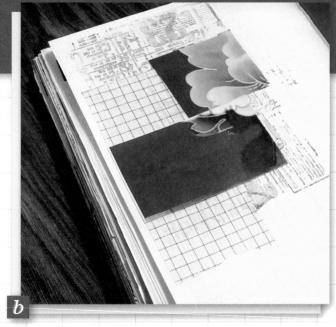

b

// I followed up by layering classic red-toned floral details over the two layers of background pattern.

c

// I added a favorite picture of a girl and kept the colors harmonious. The girl is the visual center of the page.

d

// Adding tape and stamps helps to integrate the elements with the flower picture and enhances their connections.

02

How to Make a Collage with a Decorative Secondary Element

The secondary element is the coordinator of a layout, connecting the colors of blocks and the relationships among elements.

a

// A page with only main elements is a little dull.

b

// After adding secondary elements, the page has a wealth of details and colors.

c

// Green tape strips and worded tape strips are added to the right of the page.

d

// Combining the elements of seals, stamps, and tape strips to the left of the main element enriches its content.

A Secondary Element Can Be Used Alone Without Decorating the Main Element

// The secondary element is on the upper-right corner of page. The red tape strip, number sticker, and retro patterns overlap. The red strip corresponds and connects with the red bouquet.

// The secondary element is in the lower right corner. The red retro patterns are the same as the pattern of the strips on the upper left corner, integrating the two. With the addition of the flower seal and memos enriching the secondary elements, the design is exquisite.

B.
A Secondary Element Can Be Used Alone

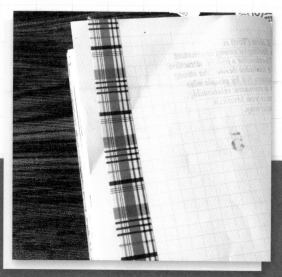

// The red tape strip on the left page is used by itself as the secondary element. It responds to the colors of the main element and unifies the elements of layout.

// The seal on the upper-left corner of the page is used as the single secondary element. It functions as a framework that determines a margin around the layout, even without clear lines.

03

Enhancing Transparency by Using Tracing Paper

Tracing paper enhances the sense of layering in a collage. Because of its translucency, even when printed, it allows the elements below it to show through.

Tracing paper is thin and translucent and achieves a delightful effect as background shading of collage.

// The flower printed on tracing paper is glued over strips and newspaper where words and color can be seen through it dimly. Tracing paper can imply a sense of layers.

04

Tearing Materials by Hand, Casually and Arbitrarily

The irregularity and haphazardness of hand-tearing pieces of newspaper, magazine pages, and tape can add a fresh and interesting element to a collage.

// The red element on the upper-left corner of the page is torn by hand. The red element is more casual and vivid than the red frame cut with scissors.

05

Boldly Dividing a Beautiful Element into Two

People are reluctant to destroy a beautiful flower or an intact picture, but sometimes a spread may be more harmonious and integrated when an element is divided into two and positioned in different sections.

// The yellow rose is divided into two as the background shading and positioned individually on either side of the spread.

Interesting Accessories in a Notebook

Sometimes the photos, pictures, and receipts we want to use don't work with the layout, or we discover that the spread is not large enough for the things we want to include. When these things happen, we can add inserts and accessories to the notebook.

01

Inserts

An insert is a page added to a notebook, sometimes for decoration, sometimes for an overflow of photos, sometimes for adding postcards, and sometimes just for fun. I usually attach my inserts into notebooks with tape or glue.

// I deliberately made the insert (with Mona Lisa and the blue-pattern background) smaller than the page size to show off the yellow color of the element at top right.

// The illustration on the reverse side of insert. Keep the colors of the insert and page below it harmonious.

// This insert is a postcard I collected and attached to the notebook.

// The bright red flower glued behind an inserted page, gives it an immediate boost.

02

Extended Pages

Generally, extended pages are added to the left and right margins of pages. They are attached with tape strips, or covered with pictures or other elements. When a page is not wide enough to accommodate the contents, an extended page can do the trick.

// Because this spread uses a large area of collage, I add an extended page to make the layout entertaining.

// The extended page accommodates many pictures that I wanted to include in the notebook. The largest picture is placed vertically on the extension.

// When I find a picture that is too large to be glued on a page, I use an extended page to fold the picture into the notebook.

// Here is a picture of an extension folded into a notebook spread. Keep the colors harmonious.

03

Little Pockets

A small envelope can be glued to a notebook as a little pocket to hold something: pictures, tickets, receipts, or leaves and flowers that cannot be included on the page. A little pocket not only protects the small things but also makes the page interesting.

// I picked up this ginkgo leaf in the autumn. Since it was too fragile to glue, I placed it in the little envelope that I had attached to the page.

// The receipts I collect on trips don't always match other elements on a page, so I put them in a little parchment envelope and add some decorations.

// If you have too many pictures and you don't want to add an extension page, a little pocket will work just fine in a travel journal.

// This is a travel journal recording a trip to Morocco. I added a pocket in the back of the journal and kept the extra photos and receipts there.

04

Postcards, Tickets, and Pamphlets

I want to glue all sorts of memories of my life into the notebook, including souvenir receipts, beautiful cards, and postcards. These elements are not always attractive if simply glued in by themselves, so we have to decorate them as well.

// The exchange currency bills, two pieces of white paper from my journey to Morocco, are overlapped with two pictures on the page. The bills did not look good when glued directly on the page. I added a background picture on the reverse side of the folded white page as decoration.

// When you open up the illustration on the left hand page, the receipt is shown. Kill two birds with one stone.

// A receipt for shoes appears on the right. Originally there was nothing of interest on the left, so I covered it with a magazine picture to beautify it.

// I buy a lot of cookies and don't want to throw away the little cards come on the bags. I glue them to the page with a picture of a pretty girl.

Section 03

COLOR MATCHING

// Everyone has a different color sense. Retro color is a very wide category because retro style includes so many different branches. In making retro collages, I find that many colors can work, as long as they blend with the style you choose.

My Favorite Retro Colors

In my journaling process I have established any number of favorite colors that I use all the time. When I find tapes and stickers in those favored colors I buy them right away. Because I use them frequently, they are reflective of the personality and "look" of my work. Some of those favorites include claret red, dark green, sapphire blue, and all shades of brown. Colors that I avoid, because of their brightness include white, pink, mint green, and light blue.

01

Retro Colors by My Destination

FEATURE 1: Pure color muted with a darker color

These three rows of colors are variations on yellow, green, blue, and red. The top row represents the original shades. In my collages, I often choose colors from the second and third rows, which are darker and more muted than the originals. Often, these "heavier" colors will make collage work appear more balanced and nuanced.

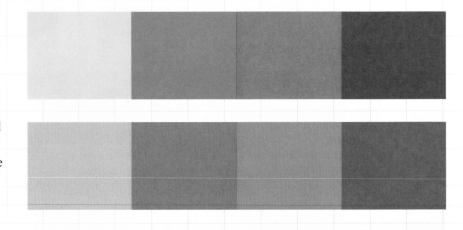

// These two French posters from the early twentieth century have intense retro styling. The colors are highly saturated but muted overall. I think a little bit of black ink has been added to the colors, which make them appear dense and dusky, with the weight of history.

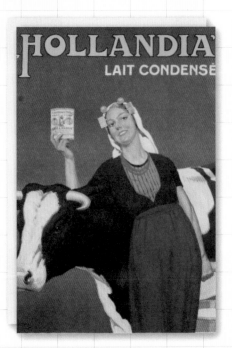

FEATURE 2: Hazy, grayed, softened colors

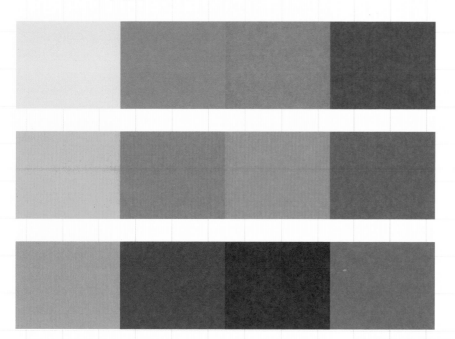

In these three rows of yellow, green, red, and blue you can see how the colors in the second two rows are gradually grayer than the originals. These grayed and softened colors give a feeling of elegance, ease, and a distinctive density. Using these colors in journaling and collage gives the work a soothing, vintage quality.

// These posters are the work of the nineteenth-century Czech illustrator and graphic artist Alphonse Maria Mucha. The colors that Mucha chose create a hazy effect. His backgrounds and tones are grayish with low purity and convey a sense of age.

The two rows of brown tones that I selected randomly are close to orange and red. Brown tones can make people feel nostalgic and warm. They serve a connecting role in journaling, matching easily with other colors, reducing the incongruity of colors, and balancing with intense contrasting colors.

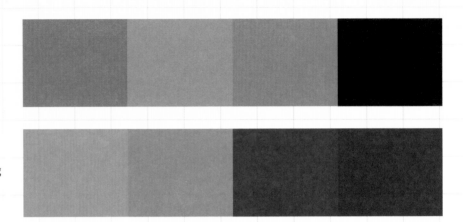

// In these two Parisian posters from the early twentieth century, the one on the left has intense color, and the one on the right is soft. Browns predominate in both, and give them an intense retro feel. In my view, browns are a visual link with history and nostalgia. When we see these tones, we naturally sense an old-world feeling.

02
My Frequently Used Colors

I like to try every color, but only a few of them end up being used frequently. Certain colors become favorites not only for their usability, but because they define my personal collage style. Below, I've featured four of the colors I use frequently in my collages—and I've given them the names that I like to use for them: Christmas red, rainforest green, Van Gogh blue, and caramel brown.

A.
Christmas Red

Christmas red is brighter than claret red and denser than pure red. I often match it with brown, yellow, and black. On a page, red is a forward color, creating a visual sense that it is coming toward you. It can lighten a page, and also draw the viewer's attention, creating a look that is memorable, intense, and sometimes shocking.

B.
Rainforest Green

Rainforest green is the color of tropical rainforest. I am extremely fond of this impressive color. On a page, I often match it with bright yellow, brown, and red, creating a sense of eternal summer. Rainforest green can not only balance the structure of a layout but can also make the page feel soft or solid.

C.
Van Gogh Blue

Van Gogh blue is the color that he used in his painting of *Branches of an Almond Tree in Blossom*. It's neither dense nor dusky, but it's very attractive. I like matching it with black and white, or tone-on-tone colors in the background. It is also enticing, when used occasionally to contrast with small areas of yellow. This blue is suitable for large area on a page for its soothing and classical charm.

D.
Caramel Brown

Caramel brown is a sweet color that reminds me of the delightful taste of caramel macchiato with marshmallows. Bright as it is, caramel brown doesn't have high saturation and it creates a sense of softness, elegance, and grace. It is easy to match with other colors, and works in both large and small areas as decoration.

My Methods of Color Matching

Color matching is one of the key parts of journaling. Because colors and styles vary from one element to another, figuring out how to match the colors well and distinctively becomes a bit tricky for many journalers.

In most cases, people look at each element individually instead of matching them with other elements when putting together a collage. That may be where color matching goes wrong for some.

When friends have asked me why their designs appear messy, the problem has often been that they have used too many colors in the same collage. This can lead to disorder and a lack of focus.

I like studying color and trying all kinds of color matching. Through experimentation, I have gradually absorbed the tricks and laws of good color matching and usually use my own color vocabulary to describe the process. But there are several classic methods of color matching that may help you: analogous colors, contrasting colors, complementary colors, and rainbow color scheme.

Generally I decide on the dominant color first, and then choose the tones to go with it or choose the elements to go with it. (See page 72: Specific Steps How to Start.) The second method requires choosing elements that already have the existing dominant or secondary colors. If the dominant color is not specific enough, squint your eyes and peer at the element: the predominant tone is the main color.

In most cases it's best to limit the number of colors in a collage to three. I usually have two colors as the main combination and a neutral (black, gray, brown) as a secondary color that will match with anything.

// Green and orange-brown are used as the dominant colors on page. The gray of newspaper, black of letters and light brown of tapes are all the secondary colors.

Analogous Color Scheme

In an analogous color scheme, a page will take on a unified hue with the use of two to three analogous (related) colors in the collage.

You might choose several red hues of different saturation and brightness and combine them for a red design. You can also apply two similar colors like blue and purple to the collage.

Some of my favorite analogous color matches include: yellow-green and olive-green, vermilion and orange, lilac and blue-gray.

A.

Shades of Yellow

If the dominate hue of page is yellow, I would match it with its analogous colors of orange, brown, and tangerine and intersperse these with dark green, brown, and red-brown.

EXAMPLE

Tan   Earth yellow   Pure yellow

// This page has an overall orange feel. On the left are an elegant yellow flower and bright yellow butterfly. The girl in gray between them connects and highlights the two areas of yellow. The coordinated layers make the page pleasing to the eye.

The use of tape strips in two shades of yellow, green leaves, and a seal help to soften the impact of the orange flower. In this way, the page does not appear to have too any colors.

B.
Shades of Blue

When deciding on blue as the dominant hue, I often emphasize the sense of layers with various blue colors and match analogous colors of green and navy blue. The shades of brown often serve as secondary colors.

EXAMPLE

Navy blue   Olive green   Blue-gray

// The image on this spread combines two blues and a green hue.

To the right is a page of collage. It has a black and white picture as the background, light brown words, and pictures as decorations. These neutrals are not as bright as blue and green, so they tend to balance and unify the design.

The secondary element to the left is glued with green tape strips and stamped with a blue seal. The page is clean and fresh.

02
Complementary Color Scheme

A complementary color scheme enriches a page and enhances its visual impact through the use of two contrasting colors. In choosing this kind of color matching, you might follow the laws of classic complementary pairings: red and green, blue and orange, yellow and purple. Or you can start with selecting the elements and then seek the complementary colors of the elements. Of course creating a feeling is also important in choosing your complementary color combinations. Try pink and gray, or green and orange.

Some of my favorite complementary color combinations include: aquamarine and lemon-yellow, rose red and dark green, black and white.

EXAMPLE

| Pure red | Navy blue | Khaki |

// Pure red and navy blue, pulled from the main element, contrast sharply on the page.

// Don't forget that the white background also plays a part in a complementary color scheme.

// The dense navy blue can balance the prominent red peony on the left-hand page.

// Selecting a picture dominated by khaki on the right aims at neutralizing the complementary colors of red and blue.

EXAMPLE

| Royal blue | Beige | Golden tan |

// This spread has a classic quality enhanced by the use of the complementary colors of blue and gold.

// The blue peony is a highlight to the right, responding to the blue and gold of the main element to the left. The beige color of two tape strips weakens the sharp contrast of the complementary colors.

// Humble as it is, the red seal to the left decorates the main element and enriches the layout.

EXAMPLE

Dark green Yellowish-brown Warm brown

EXAMPLE

Fuchsia Deep yellow Pinkish-gray

// This page shows chartreuse with the complementary colors of green and yellowish-brown.

// Green and yellowish-brown are abstracted from the main element to the right as the complementary colors.

// Brown and green tape strips and a green seal are applied to the secondary element to the left. At the same time I chose green ink for the written sections: because a large area is allowed for writing, the color of the ink is an important consideration.

// Purple and yellow are a classic complementary pairing. Here, the main colors of purple and brown and the secondary color of yellow make the collage bright and vivid.

// A yellow tape strip occupies a small area of the page to the left, but it catches the eye and responds to the color of the flower's pistil.

// Purple occupies a small area and yellow occupies a large area on the left of the page. The addition of light pinkish gray makes the page brighter but not gaudy.

NOTE: Be sure to balance the size of the areas of color when matching two bright colors.

03

Rainbow Color Scheme

If you find the concept of an analogous color scheme and complementary color scheme a little bit hard to grasp, you might find what I call a rainbow color scheme easier.

	Red
	Orange
	Yellow
	Green
	Indigo
	Blue
	Purple

+

	Pink

How to Use a Rainbow Color Scheme

First, repeat the names of the colors of the rainbow in your mind: red, orange, yellow, green, indigo, blue, purple, and another color of pink. This is the rainbow color scheme (as shown in the above illustration, please put the pink bar below the color column for convenience in color matching).

An analogous rainbow color scheme will pair two colors that fall next to each other in the rainbow.

Example: red and orange, orange and yellow, yellow and green, green and indigo, indigo and blue, blue and purple, purple and pink, pink and red.

A complementary rainbow color scheme pairs colors that are one, two, or three bars away from each other in the rainbow.

Example: red and yellow, red and green, red and indigo, orange and green, orange and indigo, orange and blue.

The Advantages of a Rainbow Color Scheme

A rainbow color scheme is easy to memorize; everyone can do it. When you're stumped for color matching, simply repeat the rainbow color scheme and you'll find the right colors.

Red — ⎤
An interval
of two
colors
Green — ⎦

// Select green from the rainbow color scheme as the basic color and red at an interval of two bars away. Pair red and green as the main colors in a collage.

Dark green

Vermilion

Misty gray

// Use dark green and vermilion as the main complementary colors and then select the tone-to-tone elements.

// The red rose to the left contains dark green and vermilion as do the two pictures to the right, which have been glued together and connected with tape strips. Matched with the black and white picture of a girl, the page sets off the two dominant colors without mixing many other colors.

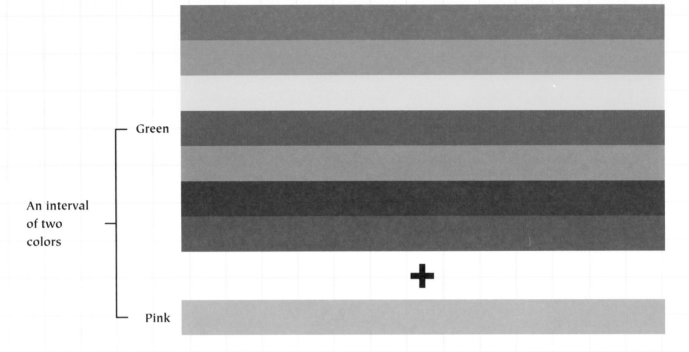

An interval
of two
colors

Green

Pink

Select green from the rainbow color scheme as the basic color, and then use it with pink in a collage.

Rainforest green

Olive green

Cameo brown

// The dominant color is pink, contrasting with a large area of green.

// The page is lively and full of energy with two different shades of green and a large area of pink.

// The black numbers and words on both sides balance the visual effect of the layout.

The Colors of the Four Seasons and Festivals

A journal records moods, feelings, and memories. Along with using pictures and words, the use of color is an interesting way to record life, and recalls the changes in seasons and traces of time in a notebook.

It is a delightful thing to record the specific colors of festivals and anniversaries, such as the red and green of Christmas, pumpkin yellow of Thanksgiving day, king red of New Years. All of these can be collected in the journal.

01

Yellow and Green of Early Spring

Spring teems with life. Writing about spring in your journal can reflect that vigorous and animated time of year. Use the color of sprouts to record the vitality in your notebook.

The pictures taken on a spring outing are good journaling elements. The colors of nature not only retain the memory of spring, but add the fresh breath of new life into your notebook.

// For this season, I will glue light yellow, bright yellow, emerald, and light green elements to the notebook.

02

Luxuriance of Summer

Entering into summer, grass and trees are blooming and luxuriant. The color of the journal will now change with the season. There will be fewer immature yellows, more mature blues, and the leaves will change from light to dark green.

// In this season, one of my frequently used colors is bluish green, which brings a cool and refreshing feeling to summer.

03

Red and Yellow Maple Leaves of Late Autumn

Autumn is the season of harvest. Leaves turn from dark green to yellow, and as they fall they turn brown. Some of the elements you can include in your journal at this time of year are photos from an autumn trip, fallen maple leaves, and letters written with brown ink.

// In this season, I will choose reddish brown and yellowish brown elements, especially tapes and seals with these colors.

04

White Snow of Midwinter

Winter in my journal takes on a light gray-blue which is reflected by snow on the ground. Since there is no way to keep snow in the journal, collect the colors of snow.

// In this season, I collect elements with a sense of winter, like cold gray and cold blue. My ink also changes to blue.

05

Festival—Red and Green of Christmas

A sense of ritual can be displayed in a journal during festivals. Before and after Christmas, I add red and green Christmas elements to my journal.

// The Christmas elements are of the characteristic type. You can include actual pine needles in a collage or draw them on the page to create the festival atmosphere.

Trying a New Kind of Color Matching and Expressing a Personal Style

01

Adding Personal Colors

Journal writing is about private memories and expression of personal style. Although there are characteristics to a retro color scheme, everyone has different preferences for color choices. In collage works, personal color matching has its own distinctive features.

// A muted pink is mixed with water colors to match the gray color on the page. Pink and gray are my favorite colors.

02

Keeping an Eye on Harmonious Color Matching in Life

Keep an eye on life and you'll find many beautiful and harmonious color matchings. The decoration of specialty stores on the street, the colors on pamphlets and natural random colors—a book, a sweater or a cup—can bring your new inspirations.

Shades of Yellow

// The bouquet shows me how to match orange, yellow, or green.

// A leather stool on a roadside in Morocco against the blue background. This matching of light blue, dark green, and brick red inspired me.

// A line of pots outside a museum are deep blue, orange-red, and light brown which takes my breath away.

// The postbox on the street of a Shanghai French concession gives me the idea for matching green and gold.

03

My Crazy Inspiration Journals

Maybe everyone, including me, is confused sometimes by colors that are easier to perceive on their own than they are together. And so we hesitate to use them in a collage.

So, I keep what I call an inspiration journal to collect all sorts of fantastic and inspiring color ideas. I can do whatever matching, collage, and painting I like in this draft journal. I don't have to worry here about bad matches.

Putting aside unnecessary worries, I can experiment with matching colors and elements that I'm not quite ready to apply in my journal. By doing this, I come up with some unexpectedly wonderful matches.

// This was inspired by the bouquet on the above page. Dark green elements are matched with orange-yellow and orange-red as the background colors. The light golden plant makes the page full of bright radiance.

// I want to try matching red and green, so I use a large area of green color as the background, contrasting it with a small area of red and matched with bronze gold.

// A stamped overlay of feather patterns coordinates the elements and adds to the visual impact.

Section 04

CONTENT RECORDINGS

At present, I have six journals, a weekly journal for to-do lists as reminders; a diary journal with a page for each day (I often slip up, several days for one page); a book journal for jotting down my favorite passages and recording my feelings; a movie journal for recording the deep impressions and feelings some movies inspire in me; a travel journal for recording my travel memories and keeping receipts and pictures; an inspiration journal for recording my crazy ideas and random collages and doodling.

Weekly Journals

My weekly journal is used to record to-do lists. I make notes of the important things I need to do every day and tick them when they are done.

01

Weekly Journals Available in Shops

// I use a Hobonichi weekly journal.

// This is what the Hobochici journal looks like inside.

// Every week, I record my to-do list on the left and write down things that I think are important in the right.

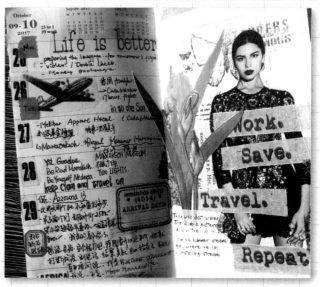

// Sometimes I also use a weekly journal as a travel notebook. A TN's layout is similar to that of a weekly journal: The left page is divided into seven sections for recording daily events, and the right page leaves a large area of blank space for free design.

02
Drawing Your Own To-Do List Page in the Weekly Journal

You can design your own to-do list page in an ordinary notebook based on the amount of space you need for the things you do each day. Drawing your own to-do lists gives you more flexibility to accommodate changes and different layouts.

I'll show you the steps for creating a to-do list page.

Preparation tools:
1. A5 notebook
2. Acrylic stamp block
3. Ruler
4. Needle pen
5. Clear rubber stamp
6. Number seal
7. Inkpad

// First, open to a blank page. Draw the grids for seven days with a fine pen and ruler, adjusting the layout to ensure that each part of the grid has enough space.

// Stamp a number seal on the appropriate grids. In the upper left, stamp the calendar and name of the month.

c

// In the lower right, draw a frame for recording important events for the week or any contents that needs highlighting. Use a marker to highlight the present week on the calendar.

d

// Decorate the white space with clear rubber stamps. I used plant stamps for my decorations. Place the stamp on an acrylic stamp block, then press the block on the notebook page, arranging the composition as you like.

e

// Decorate the left side of the calendar appropriately, using a clear rubber stamp.

NOTE: After use, a clear rubber stamp should be stored flat against the plastic board to keep it safe and prolong its use.

f

// In the lower right, draw a frame for recording important events for the week or any content that needs highlighting. Use a marker to highlight the present week on the calendar.

g

// Fill the grids with everyday to-do lists and tick them off or cross them out when they are done. You can record important events in the box on the right-hand page for easy reference.

NOTE: A loose-leaf notebook can also be used for weekly journaling. That way you can add or delete pages as required, and it's also convenient to carry.

Diary Journals

My diary journal is mainly for recording interesting and valuable trifles in daily life. Sometimes I'll fill a whole page, recording events or writing down my feelings, without any special composition. When I don't want to write, I will fill the page with collages or paintings.

Here is a motivating note I've been including in my journals, "Don't give yourself too many rules or require daily records. Enjoying the process of journaling is the important thing—the choice of what to write or how to decorate a page is up to you."

I want my diary journal to be a record of little things in my life and my daily mood, instead of pursuing a full-page or beautiful journal.

// Print some informal photos from your daily life, glue them into the book and record the contents of the photos beside them. This way of recording is simple and can be used as a great memory aid. I like to record things that are often overlooked, such as cute teacups, handy notes in books, and so on.

// When I find interesting varieties of paper, I stick them in my notebook for later use. The piece of rough, light brown paper is my coffee filter! I tore a piece of it to write on in my journal.

// I also keep a record of the art works I create in a page-a-day diary. This is the decoration for a Christmas bell made with embossing powder and a heat gun. I cut it out and saved it in the notebook.

// Polaroid pictures in the diary. Retro-style cinematic photographs of summer become a natural decorative element on the pages.

Book Journals

I read a lot of paperback books and I like to jot down favorite phrases and passages from them. I also like to write down the feelings that I have when I read, and the dates when I read books. My book journal is a collection base for knowledge. There are some book journals commercially available, such as the one by Moleskine, which lists various topics for your records.

You can also design your own book journal, composing the layout to suit your own needs for the kinds of books you read and the things that are important for you to record.

My book journal includes reading summaries, records of my monthly reading habits, records of my annual reading habits, book lists, and more.

01
Book Journals Available in Shops

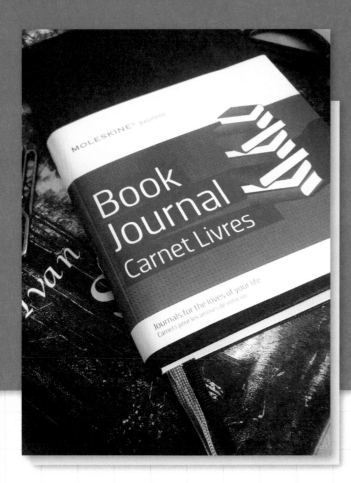

// Here is a Moleskine book journal. I used this type of notebook when I first started journaling. It is a good choice if you simply want to jot down notes, or for anyone who doesn't enjoy designing layouts.

// In this journal, two books can be recorded on each spread. The designer has labeled the information that needs to be recorded, such as author, publication date, title of the book, and so on. The area at the bottom of each page is for quotations and impressions. The areas are distinguished by different colors. This layout is well suited for systematic reading and recording.

Book Journal with the Layout Drawn by Yourself: Different Contents for Recording in Different Ways

In a blank notebook, plan out the kind of layout you need for different information categories.

First plan what is to be recorded, then glue pictures in the notebook as you write. Don't glue all the pictures on the page at the same time or you might run out of text space.

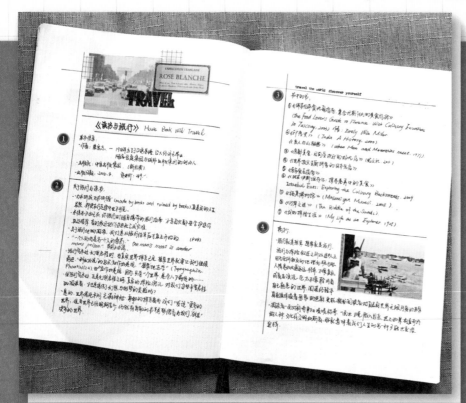

// The basic information for book journaling includes: author, publisher, publishing date, price, page count, and so on.

Interesting points about the book you're reading, the information in it, and extended reading can also be recorded in your journal. This is a convenient way to keep information systematized for easy reference.

// When I read Van Gogh's Letters: *The Mind of the Artist in Paintings, Drawings, and Words*, I printed Van Gogh's paintings and manuscripts and added them to the journal.

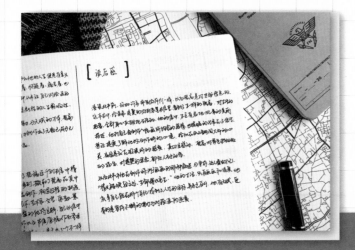

// On a large page, the text can be arranged in two columns, which makes reading easier.

// One thing that is important to me is writing down my personal thoughts about the book I'm reading. Every book has a different impression on me. I jot down two sentences about my feelings and understanding of the book. This can be very helpful to me when I go back and read what I wrote later.

// If you are interested in specific areas of content, you can add it to the relevant reading section at the end of your reading notes. This can be very helpful in building your reading system.

03

Reading Summary Form

Arranging booklists is one of my favorite things to do. This kind of summary record in a journal is clear and concise, and does not need too many decorations.

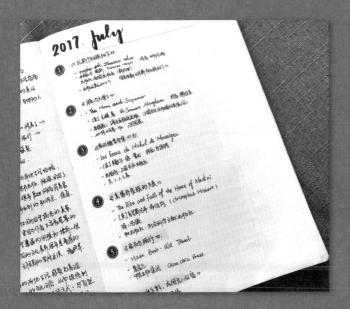

// This is my booklist from July of 2017. I read six books that month. I did my book journaling and simply listed the basic information, such as the names of the book and author.

// This page is a summary of my annual booklist for 2017. The list clearly shows my whole year's booklists, and the name and number are also clear.

Film Journals

To my way of thinking, keeping a book journal is mainly for recording my reading list and jotting down favorite passages and quotations. A film journal, for me, is more about recording my feelings and impressions about films. I use the journal to save the things I want to remember about the film, rather than recording who I saw it with, and when. I hope that when I open my journal, years from now, I'll recall how I felt not only through what I wrote, but through beautiful and vivid pages.

01

Films Journal Available in Shops

// This is Moleskine's film journal, which details the information needed to be fill in. A spread can record two movies.

// Because I like to match content with images, I usually use a spread to record one film instead of two.

// If you go to the cinema to watch the film, save the ticket and glue it in the journal.

// This is also a Moleskine film journal that is divided into two sections, one for the basic information about the movie and the other for thoughts and impressions. Generally I don't write the review for every film I have watched. I only do that for my favorites and the illuminating ones.

02

The Tricks of Drawing the Layout for a Film Journal

My journal contains any number of pictures, so the selection and position of pictures is essential.

In the selection of pictures, I make every effort to keep the color and style of the collage elements harmonious with those of the movie. I also try to keep the pictures the same size, for a concise and unified layout design.

// Here, the two spreads rely mainly on retro pink. This is my film journaling of *The Grand Budapest Hotel*. The text is aligned with the pictures and matched with the white space.

// Here are two spreads of journaling for the film *Scent of a Woman*. When there are many images from a film that you want to glue into the book, follow the example of the book on the right where 8 pictures of the same size are arranged neatly.

// I added my favorite poster to the page and adjusted it to the page-size when printed. This kind of layout is elegant and balanced.

// This is my film journaling of *Still Walking*. The name, director, actors, and reviews are placed on different pages for clarity.

// As shown in the left and right illustrations, the tape strips are used to separate the content and decoration. The patterns of tapes should not be complex since film pictures are rich enough. Whenever you lack layout inspiration, you can refer to your favorite magazine layout.

Travel Journals

In every travel I will prepare a notebook which is a travel journal. Usually one notebook is for one destination or one travel. The chosen notebook is easily-carried. Whatever I saw and heard in the journey at night are recorded on it and the elements collected are glued to the page.

01

Your Personal Travel Journal

A traveler's notebook, or TN for short, is the type of travel journal I use most frequently. I like it not only for the retro leather cover, but also for the convenience of being able to add or delete inserts. There are many types of inserts available, but no more than six can be used at once.

// The passport size and standard TNs are used most often. The passport is more suitable for carrying with you every day.

// In traveling, I often carry only an insert and cover, which are portable and small. In addition, the pages of one insert are often enough for a whole trip or destination.

02
What Can be Recorded in a Travel Journal

// Here is the opening page of a travel journal where the date and destination of the trip are recorded as embellishments.

// Before traveling, I write out a detailed list of the things I will need to pack and then prepare accordingly. This way I won't forget!

// Before the trip, I write down travel tips, arrangements, and some dos and don'ts in the journal, one page for each day. Maps can be glued on the pages for reference.

// Tourist attraction tickets, business cards, and some interesting sticky notes also can be kept in the notebook.

// Plane tickets and rail tickets are kept as souvenirs and glued to the page. If the layout is too simple, you can add tape strips as decorations.

// Basic information about famous tourist attractions and museums can be collected and recorded in the journal as travel tips for reference on the journey.

// Brochures from tourist attractions can be kept in the notebook as souvenirs. If the brochure is too long, simply fold it under. (See page 92.)

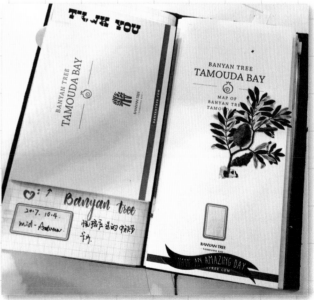

// Sometimes you may come across charming little surprises such as a blessing card prepared by a hotel for the Mid Autumn Festival, a pretty hotel map, and other delicate pieces that are indispensable parts of your journey.

// After your trip, print your photos and glue them into the notebook.

// As shown in the illustrations, the pages are designed with tone-on-tone colors. The photos are printed with high-quality printing paper instead of photographic paper since the latter is too thick and will make the notebook hard to close.

03

A Storage Bag for Travel Journaling Tools

// This is a storage bag for journaling tools when I travel. I wrap various tape strips around two or three pieces of board and attach other tapes and stickers to release paper. This makes everything compact, leaves room for other materials, and is easy to carry.

// My storage bag is a handbag. When I travel I outfit it with one or two pens, a small pair of scissors, a dot liner, and a small draft book that can hold my travel lists and accommodation notes.

NOTE: Journalers who like to paint in their notebooks can add a few simple painting tools to their travel bag. Don't carry too many decorative materials with you. Usually I simply glue a few collected materials onto the pages as I write the text while I travel. Then I add the tapes and decorations and photos when the trip is over.

Don't forget, you can add inserts and page extensions (see pages 89-90) if you need extra room for content.

Inspiration Journals

Every time I start a new journal, I spend a lot of time choosing my elements and planning layouts; worries about whether or not my collages will work can make me hesitant about starting. I think a lot of us have this problem. To work around it, I have a notebook I call my "Inspiration Journal" where I design collages randomly.

In this book I can be fearless about the collages I paste on the pages, the patterns I draw, and the tools and techniques I use for creating them.

My inspiration journal is the notebook I devote to recording my creative thoughts and artistic experiments. When creative new ideas come to mind, this journal is where I record them.

An inspiration journal is a place where I can put my inspiration into action and constantly exert my imagination and creativity. Through this process, I come across harmonious color matchings and ways to match elements of various styles. Of course, it's also a pleasure. As time goes by, the creative layouts and collage artworks develop as my personal style.

01

Collecting Collage Inspiration in a Cast-off Notebook

My first inspiration book was a Hobonichi diary in 2016. At that time, I wrote in the diary intermittently for two weeks, and then put it aside. During the summer vacation, I happened to find this book and wanted to reuse it, so I began to add collage to the pages I had written on earlier.

In the collage process, because I wanted to cover up the text, I simply added elements to each page without worrying about arrangement and design.

After two weeks of covering the pages of a diary with images, I realized that the random collages I had created were just as interesting as the ones that I put together after a lot of thinking. So I continued collaging randomly until the diary was full.

// This is what my first inspiration book looked like when it was full. I added a leather cover to protect it.

// This is my favorite collage in my first inspiration journal.

02

Interesting Experiments in My Inspiration Journal

There is no need to find a particular type of notebook for an inspiration journal. Any notebook can become your own inspiration notebook. Whether the collage is good or bad, it can stay in the book. By looking through an inspiration notebook, you will be able to see your progress in collage and journaling.

As you experiment boldly in the book, you may have some happy surprises. For example, after painting with a watercolor pen, try dripping water over the paint to make the colors blur. Or you might use pens that produce different effects to create a fantastic flower.

// On these pages, I used blue and green marker pens to draw flowers and leaves freely, then I added a little water to blur the pattern.

// The blurred color was a beautiful discovery that resulted from my experiment. Because there is not much water, the outlines of some flowers and leaves remain the same.

// I like the semi-blur state of this page which gives a light hazy feeling to the collage.

// In my inspiration notebook, I often use different pens to draw strange plants.

// The flower patterns are drawn with three types of coloring tools: gel-ink pen, watercolor, and crayon create a fresh and unique look, which is my favorite painting mode.

Experiments with New Color Matching in the Inspiration Journal

My favorite way to practice successful color matching is to try out the combinations first in the inspiration journal. Sometimes it's impossible to imagine what a color match will look like. Only when they are painted or pasted, can you really sense whether the colors are harmonious or not.

We all have our own preference for color combinations, but you might not recognize them all until you try them out. You can do that with confidence in the inspiration book and find your favorite color matches and style.

// I came across the color match of dark green and orange accidentally, But since then, I've used it frequently in collages.

// Azure and rose are both colors with high saturation—too strong to be a good color match for me. I haven't used it in collage since experimenting with it here—it helped me discover my own style.

04

Practicing Handwriting with Collage in an Inspiration Journal

I like trying out different English writing styles, but I worry about actually using it on pages.

I often practice new typefaces in the inspiration journal. Sometimes I design the background first and then write the letters. Sometimes I write the letters first and then add a background picture.

// First I filled the page with light blue and light pink, and then randomly wrote the letters in different sizes to fill up the page.

// After writing the words in green, I thought the page looked a little empty, so I added the pink watercolor. You can leave white space, or create a blurred ink effect about the text.

Section 05

SKILLS TO IMPROVE YOUR JOURNAL

// Along with decorating pages with stickers, tapes, and seals, you can also add small illustrations or include other handiwork in your notebooks. For example you might want to stamp a handmade seal, draw pictures of the delicious snacks you have eaten while traveling, or experiment with retro sealing wax.

// These small skills can enrich the journal, increase the joy of keeping records, and reflect your own best journal style.

// In my three years of my journaling, I have learned to do simple watercolor painting, to carve rubber seals, and to seal letters and gifts with sealing wax, so these skills are not unattainable.

Drawing Simple Watercolor Illustrations

When I had just begun to get into journaling, I thought I'd like to draw illustrations of favorite things on the pages, so I started to practice watercolor painting. What I paint most in my book are flowers and leaves.

I have a watercolor journal that contains the images of plants that I've painted in different periods. With each painting, I've also recorded notes about how I mixed the colors and my painting process. Keeping my notes about process along with the painting in the notebook makes it a convenient way to learn, when I go back and look at what I've done.

// These are the flower and fruits I painted in my watercolor journal.

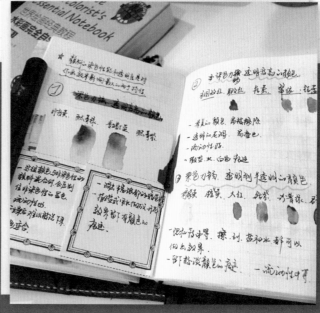

// This page lists the methods and key points about my watercolor methods.

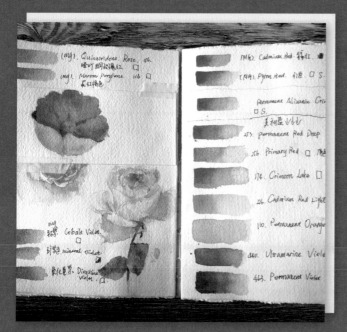

// When I practice drawing a plant, I also record my color matching.

// This page keeps a record of the process of mixing colors and my favorite colors.

Watercolor Paper and Watercolor Journals

A.
Watercolor Paper

Materials

• Classification—Wood pulp and rag paper

• Characteristics—Wood pulp has poor water absorption and does not diffuse paint well. The paper is smooth, and although it leaves water marks, it can also make color very visual.

Rag paper is made from 100% cotton rag, so it is more expensive than wood paper and has good water absorption.

• Applicability—Wood pulp is suitable for elegant and fresh illustrations, such as small paintings of food in a travel journal, small landscapes, and other small illustrations.

Rag paper is suitable for diffusion and mixing colors, but it is rough, very grainy, and slightly yellow. It is appropriate for painting larger figures and landscapes.

Texture

• Type—Hot-pressed, cold-pressed and rough

• Applicability—Hot-pressed paper is suitable for painting plants, and cold-pressed and rough paper are suitable for landscape painting.

Weight

• Definition—Weight here refers to the thickness of watercolor paper, which is usually shown as weight per square meter. The heavier the paper, the thicker and less apt to wrinkle it will be.

• Type—185g, 300g and 610g (according to the weight classifications of the French paper manufacturer Arches). Other brands will have different weight classifications.

*My Recommendation

The paper I use most is 300g hot or cold press Arches rag paper. It holds up well to water, is relatively easy to erase or modify, and stands up to wear and tear.

// Painted flowers on wood pulp paper   // A painted flower on rag paper

B.
Watercolor Journals

Available in different thicknesses and textures, most of the watercolor journals for sale are made from wood pulp. Rag paper journals are more appropriate for professional watercolor painting.

My Recommendation

I usually use a Moleskine watercolor journal as my inspiration journal, with inserts added for use as a TN. A journal with wood pulp paper is suitable for both watercolor and writing.

When I only paint with watercolor without any writing or collage, I use a professional rag paper watercolor book. The most common ones are 300g cold-pressed spiral-bound journal of French Arches and 300g spiral-bound journal of Lamplight of Japanese Muse. The paper in these two books is fine for watercolors in a realistic style, and the diffusion effects are not bad. But because the paper is thick and rough, it is not easy to write on. Perhaps most important, a rag paper watercolor book is expensive and not conducive to journaling.

// This is painted in a Moleskine journal of the A4 size.

// This is painted on a TN insert.

// These are painted on the 300g weight pages of a Japanese Lamplighting spiral-bound journal. The paper is appropriate for wet painting and dries slowly.

// This is painted on the 300g cold-press pages of an Arches B5 spiral-bound journal.

02

Your Own Watercolor Paints

I began learning about painting two years ago, because of journaling. Before that I didn't have any real background in painting. I've summed up what I've learned here, as basics that everyone can follow. I'm sure that many of my friends out there want to draw or paint in their journal but hesitate because they haven't studied professionally. I want to tell you, anyone can paint, so get out your notebook and paint with me.

Tools:
1. French Arches, 16k, 300g, cold-pressed watercolor paper
2. Da Vinici V35 sable hair watercolor brush set: No.000, No.3, No.6 and No.428 of Da Vinici
3. Pencil
4. Materials you need for painting
5. 24 color set of French Sennelier solid watercolors
6. Bottle for brush cleaning

// Here are two boxes of watercolors of different sizes. On the left is Sennelier's wooden box of 24 solid watercolors, which is suitable for indoor use. On the right is a metal box of 12-color solid watercolors for travel.

// When I want to paint while traveling, I bring this pair of materials with me. The solid watercolors in a steel box are convenient for use, and you can mix the colors on the white lid flaps. I also bring along a Holbein watercolor brush pen, which stores water, and is easy to use. It has a cap, and water does not leak out.

A.
Steps for Watercolor Painting—A Fallen Leaf

Fallen leaves in autumn: if you can't keep them in your journal, then paint them. Here I'll share my process for autumn leaf painting. It's easy to learn, and then you can paint leaves in your own journal.

// Use a pencil to outline the shape of the fallen leaf. Then draw the center veins of the leaf, this will help you with the later coloring.

NOTE: Use an eraser as little as possible on rag paper because it will damage the surface. You can draw your draft on scratch paper, trace over it, and duplicate it on the watercolor paper with a copier. If you've never drawn before, you can print a photo of a leaf and copy it onto a sheet of watercolor paper.

// When you've completed your outline, using a No. 6 brush (I used DaVinci V35) to paint the leaf with a thin layer of water.

// Use a wet No. 6 brush to absorb Indian yellow and French vermilion, individually. (The palette in the corner of illustration C shows Indian yellow on the left and French vermilion on the right.) Place the colors on your palette and mix them for a high degree of saturation. Start by painting just a small area of the leaf.

// Load the brush with water again and begin spreading the color slowly. When the water has thinned evenly, begin brushing from the edge of the leaf with a small amount of Indian yellow. Shift to the veins in the center of the leaf and blend the two colors.

NOTE: As far as possible, let the color mix with the flow of water. Don't use a brush to interfere with it on the paper frequently. In this way, the boundaries that they form will be more natural.

d

// While the surface of the leaf is still wet, repeat the process on the other side of the leaf. The colors should be darker near the main veins and at the bottom of the leaf.

NOTE: While you are painting, there should be less water in the paint on the brush than there is on the surface of the paper. If there is too much water on the tip of brush, the paint color will be too light and water marks will easily appear. When adding colors, if you find gaps in areas that have already dried, brush a light film of water over the area first. Try not to let new color come into contact with existing colors to avoid water marks.

e

// While the color is still wet, you can add a small amount of red ochre with a No. 3 brush (I used a DaVinci V35 watercolor pen) at the junction of the veins and the lower part of the leaf to create an illusion of depth.

// Because the paper is still wet, the amount of water in the red ochre should be less than that on the paper so that the color can mix with others.

// After finishing the first layer of color, make sure the paper is completely dry before beginning the second layer. If you want the paper to dry quickly, use a hair dryer set on "low."

NOTE: The paper must be thoroughly dried before it can be painted a second time.

f

// The second layer is colored with the No. 3 brush. This layer will add dark tones to the background to depict details and to make the bright colors of the leaf richer. The contrasts of dark and light areas creates an illusion of depth.

// Paint the veins of the leaf and the lower edge with a little red ochre and umber.

NOTE: The lines can be drawn randomly and the edges of color diffused with water.

// When you've completed the veins and shadows, use a No. 00 brush to create the mottled details of the surface. Add dots with a little warm brown to make the surface appear withered. Dots of brown added to the areas that are still damp will mix with the background. You can diffuse the dots added to dried areas with a little water to create a mottled surface. Use deep brown to detail areas of rot, diffusing the edges with water to enhance the depth of color.

This fallen leaf is done. The techniques of wet painting and dry painting are applied throughout the process. You do not use a lot of water, so journal pages, such as a TN sketch journal, should be able to stand up to the process. You can also make the painting on a postcard or a watercolor block and add it to the notebook later. Controlling the amount of water is the trickiest part of the process.

NOTE: In my experience, you need the most water for the first layer, and less with each layer after that. Don't start the second layer until the first has dried; the paint will become muddy if the color is added to the wet paper.

Carving an Eraser Stamp with a Knife

At the end of 2017, after buying a lot of seals, the germ of an idea about learning to carve eraser stamps took root in my mind. I didn't need them for anything special, I just want to produce them with my own style.

Eraser carving starts with my favorite patterns, flowers, and plants. I have read many books and watched videos about stamp carving, bought a variety of knives and rubber stamp blocks, studied and practiced for several months, and finally got the hang of it.

The process for eraser stamp carving that I will share with you doesn't have very strict steps. The sum of what I've learned in my carving process is really a simple, practical method and it only requires a single knife.

// This flower is carved using a "negative" technique, where the pencil lines of your drawing are carved away. The carved lines will be the color of the paper.

// This flower is carved using a "positive" technique, where you carve away all of the material except the pencil lines. The outlines will be the color of the ink.

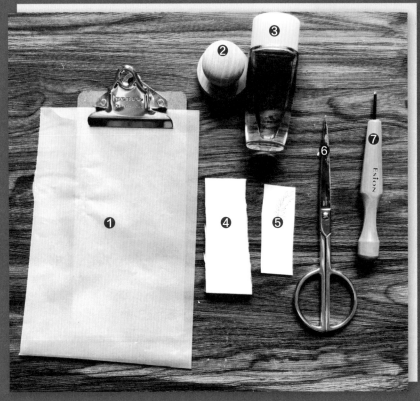

Preparation Tools:
1. Tracing paper
2. Round wooden eraser stamp handle
3. Nail polish remover
4. Eraser stamp block
5. Drawn or printed image
6. Scissors
7. Japan Esion woodcut knife (V Parting Tool, one edge length 1.5mm)

// Prepare a blank stamp block, cleaning its surface with water. Transfer the image to the stamp block. Make sure the image is smaller than the block. I chose a leaf pattern.

// Prepare a bottle of nail polish remover for the transfer.

// Lay the image face-side down on the eraser stamp block. Pour just enough nail polish remover on the paper to wet it evenly.

NOTE: Be careful in this process. Make sure the paper doesn't move as you work.

// Cover the wet paper with a piece of tracing paper and rub the tracing paper with a coin, card, or nail.

// The tracing paper prevents the nail polish remover from evaporating too quickly, and protects the paper with the image while you rub.

// Pull the paper off slowly to see if the complete graphic has transferred to the rubber stamp.

NOTE: Depending on the type of rubber stamp and nail polish remover that you use, the transferred print might be dark or it might be light. If it's a little on the light side, you can draw on top of it to make it darker.

In general, a laser printed graphic transfers better than an inkjet printed graphic. An inkjet graphic can easily smear on the rubber stamp.

NOTE: Don't over do the rubbing. It's best to rub only one or two times in one direction to make sure every area has been covered.

// Next, carve the eraser stamp with a v-parting tool. A V-parting tool is one type of rubber stamp knife. Its blade has a 30° angle, and looks like a V formed by the left and right sides. The lower edge is the central point of the V. The greater the force, the deeper the carving and the thicker the line. With less force, the lines are shallower and finer. A V-parting tool is used mainly to carve details.

e

// I can usually make an eraser stamp with only a V-parting tool. First, I use the blade to cut from the outer edge at the bottom. One edge of the blade is close to the line and moves along the track of the line.

Because this stamp will be printed with the "positive" technique, it's important to keep the outlines intact. When the blade moves, the closer it is to the junction of the line, the less force you need.

NOTE: Because the carving area is small, it's best to start from the narrow angle to ensure that the line at the angle is complete.

f

// The order of carving is as follows: first carve the most outer line of leaf, then carve the gap between each leaf, and finally carve the blanks in the leaves.

// Because the graphic of leaves is small, when the knife is inserted into the stamp, the force should be light and the angle of the knife should be slightly upward, so that the lines will be thinner.

g

h

// When the overall outline is finished, cut away the excess parts of the rubber stamp with scissors. And then use the V-parting tool to cut off the blank area around the leaves. In this way, the shape of the leaves is highlighted.

NOTE: After the preliminary carving, you can test the eraser stamp with an inkpad to see whether the lines are clear or not. Check to see if there are any forgotten or unfinished places and make corrections.

i

// Test the stamp on white paper to see the effect. I like graphics with a range of line thicknesses that, to me, suggest a hand-drawn feeling. When I carve, I give the lines different weights for a natural-looking vibrancy.

j

// Attach the stamp to the round wooden eraser stamp handle. Your DIY leaf stamp is done.

// The stamp works equally well on a journal page or a card.

Sealing Wax for Sealing Envelopes or Decorating Journals

With my love for the vintage elements, working with sealing wax was inevitable for me. It has an inherent sense of age. A sealing wax stamp is almost an icon of retro journaling since it's so historical. Sealing wax can also be used in combination with your collections of leaves, ribbons, petals, and cards in daily life. When wrapping gifts, I also use sealing wax to attach decorations. The meltable wax comes in many colors; my favorites are retro bronze gold and red.

// Attach a fallen leaf in a journal with sealing wax.

// This is a gift for my friends on Christmas. I use red sealing wax to match the Christmas berries, attach the branches, and decorate the box.

// Sealing wax also appears in my journal as a decoration.

// I keep my sealing wax stamps in an aromatherapy wax cup, which is beautiful and convenient for use.

Embossing a Trace of Time with Sealing Wax

The first function of sealing wax in history was to seal letters.

Many people like sealing wax but are afraid to try it because they think it's too complicated. In fact, sealing wax is very easy to use. There are all kinds of sealing wax available, to be melted and applied in stick form or block form, or used with a glue gun.

Preparation Tools: 1. Candle 2. Wax stamp handles 3. Wax sticks 4. Wax melting spoon 5. Scissors 6. Envelope 7. Ribbon

A.
The Steps for Using the Sealing Wax Stamp—Sealing Letters

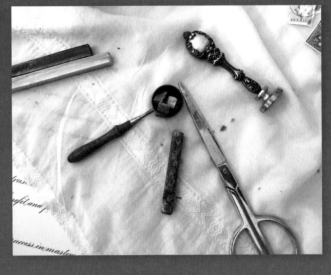

// After putting the finished letter into the blue envelope, I cross wrap it with a blue ribbon. The ribbons cross at the triangular opening of the envelope.

NOTE: The ribbon here can also be replaced by fine thread or string. I prefer to wrap the envelope with the silk ribbon.

// Choose colors that match the letter and ribbon. I choose the gold stick, then cut small pieces from it, and put the pieces in the spoon.

// The amount of sealing wax that you put in the spoon depends on the size of the stamp. The larger the stamp, the more sealing wax you will need.

// Hold the spoon over a candle flame and slowly melt the wax.

// The sealing wax is apt to have lumps as it melts. I stir it in the spoon, using the remaining stick of wax as my stirrer.

// When the wax has melted, hold the spoon over the envelope and pour it slowly over the junction in the ribbon.

NOTE: Pour slowly, dispersing the wax around the ribbon crossing as much as possible.

// Press the stamp into the wax before it sets up. Let the stamp remain in place briefly. Remove the stamp when the wax solidifies.

// After removing the stamp, you can see what the seal looks like. Because the ribbon is not flat, the seal will not be perfectly symmetrical, but it is good to have the ribbon embedded in the wax.

// Finally, cut the vertical section of ribbon short to make a small bow, and add a decorative stamp or two. Insert a small card with the recipient's name on the front of the envelope. The envelope with the sealing wax stamp is done.

// Here is a close up of the sealing wax stamp.

Chapter 3

JOURNALING
AND LIFE

• Organizing Journaling Objects
• Journaling Attitudes in Life

Notebook, tape, folder, and graphic…All of these small, ordinary objects bring me happiness, they add sparkle to my life. They hover between my desk and cabinet and expand my world. Even when life is difficult, the happy accidents and inspired moments that come with journaling save me from it.

Section 01

ORGANIZING JOURNALING OBJECTS

In my three years of journaling, one of the trickiest things for me was figuring out how to store my journaling tools and materials. Notebooks, tapes, seals, printed graphics, small stickers, binders and folders—all of these things crowd my desk, my cabinet, and the entire room. Since I love to collect and buy journaling supplies, I needed to figure out a way to sort them out and keep the room in order.

// My desk and all the stuff on it in the spring of 2018

Organizing Journaling Materials and Tools

For storing journaling tools and materials, it is important to group and organize them logically. From day to day, because I love these materials, I'm constantly buying and collecting more. If they are not arranged well, they not only take up too much space, but they also create a mess. Organized storage can help us find what we need and save time, even when there is a lot of stuff.

In my experience, organized storage meets these three conditions: it saves space, it helps you find things easily, and it's economically and environmentally sound: There is no need to go out and buy a bunch of boxes for storage.

Notebooks,tapes, stickers, seals, pens, inks, pigments, collaging tools—all need to be sorted out and stored. I have summarized some practical tips for storage below. I hope they help you solve your storage problems.

01

Arranging Picture Materials Is Very Important

In the earlier chapters, I shared the various kinds of materials I collect with you. These include: printed pictures, newspaper and magazine pictures, and other assortments. I used to spend a lot of time and energy keeping them organized by type, size, and quality. If they are not put in order, many good materials will be forgotten or you'll spend a lot of time searching for them.

After trying a lot of different ways of organizing my materials and comparing the pros and cons, I summarized the best methods. I'll share them with you here.

// The Chinese materials I've collected

A.
Common Binder for Collecting Paper Materials

One of my most frequently-used folders for holding materials is a binder, with two holes, pockets, and inserts. It has about 20 pages, which meets most of my needs. I'll tell you about two ways that I use binders.

Bind in the plastic sleeves designed for stamp and coin collections, and organize your materials by style, color, and pattern.

Many of my materials are photos and pictures downloaded and printed from the Internet. If paper materials of different sizes are folded and kept in the pockets, it's hard to find favorite pattern when I need it. Thus, all materials should be visible, face up, and the transparent sleeves with pockets of different sizes designed for stamp and coin collections are the best choices.

There are a variety of clear plastic inserts available that are made especially for use in binders. The inserts are designed with pockets of different sizes, designed for holding postcards, photos, postage stamps, and other small pieces securely. These will allow you to place photos and other items in individually, or to overlap them— and yet still be able to see them. And they will allow you to easily remove the items for use when you need them.

When materials are classified according to style, color, and pattern, it is easier to find the pictures you want to use and it saves a lot of time.

// Here is a page from a loose leaf binder where pictures of the same style are gathered together.

// In this spread from a loose leaf binder, I collected pictures of the same color.

// This page in the binder is my collection of words and phrases.

// I also collect stamps that I like.

Since binders are usually very thick, I make two holes with a hole punch in the bottom of the bags and keep them in the binder. Each bag contains one type of material. I put my small and scattered materials in small bags; large materials in large bags. According to your own needs, bags can be added or deleted.

// The blue bag includes numbered and labeled materials.

// Each file is independent and can be added or removed.

Way Comparison

	Characteristics of Collected Materials	Applicability	Advantage	Disadvantage
Adding Inserts of Stamp or Coin Album to Binder	Complete picture materials	Daily pictures, magazine images, and full-page pictures form newspapers and printed pictures	1. Easy and convenient to search for materials 2. Easy to take out materials	Not easy to carry with you
Adding File Bag to Binder	Cut up of or oversize paper	1. Small bag: leftover materials 2. Big bag: Big printed materials and the complete pages torn from magazine	1. Logical classification and proper organization 2. Easy to carry with you	Cost a lot of time to find materials

NOTE: You can combine these two methods to keep your materials organized. If you have lots of varied supplies, add transparent pocketed sleeves to your binder for some items and a clear bag for other loose materials.

B.
An Expanding File Folder for Collecting Materials

When I have a lot of printed materials and paper to organize, I use expanding file folders along with the binder and bags we've already discussed.

The advantages of an expanding file folder is that its many layered pockets make it easy to group and classify materials. I usually put printed materials of different qualities in the file folder, one pocket for each type. Sometimes I print more materials than I need at one time, but not all the materials are cut out immediately. (Don't cut too many materials at one time. The smaller the material is, the more it is apt to scatter and get lost.) These full-sheet A4 size materials will be sorted and put into the expanding file folder and taken out when they are needed.

I also put complete newspapers and special paper materials in the expanding file folder.

// Here are two kinds of expanding file folder that I use now.

// I stick labels to each layer for easy research.

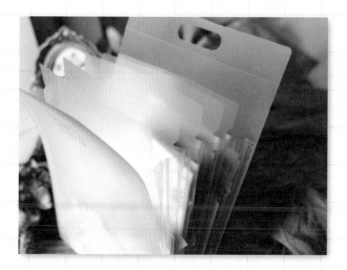

// This is what a vertical expanding file folder looks like when it is packed fully with materials.

// This is a horizontal expanding file folder that contains my collection of complete newspaper and magazine materials.

The Storage of Stamps, Notebooks, Seals, and Stickers

When I started journaling, I bought a few tapes and seals and kept them in a small wood box or metal tray.

Wooden boxes with dividers are suitable for sorting and grouping cut materials, making it easy to find the pieces you want to use. When I only have a few items, I keep them on the desk, handy for journaling at any time. Having my tools and materials visible is not only practical, but ornamental.

// I keep commonly used tapes in this nicely designed plate on my desk.

// I use this small wooden divided box to store seals. Seals of different shapes and sizes are placed in different compartments.

// I use the various wooden boxes shown here to store tapes, stickers, and seals.

// It is very practical to store all kinds of cut materials in a wooden divided box.

A.
The Storage of Tapes

Daily Storage

My tapes are kept in an A4-sized file box. This is by far the most convenient and practical way for me to store them.

First of all, I categorize tapes according to the pattern, roughly dividing them into: strip, receipt, plant, text, number, single pattern, and others. Each type is loaded into a file box.

If you buy too many tapes of one kind and they don't all fit in one place, just start a new box. Labeling and writing the type of tape on each box can help you distinguish them easily. Each of these boxes is sold separately, so they can be purchased in quantities according to your own needs. When placed on the desk, they can also be stacked or arranged as you like, which makes storage very flexible and convenient. Tapes can be placed vertically in the box to save space. The height of the box is suitable for more tapes, but if you have one that is too deep, simply lay it on its side, as shown.

// The tapes lie in the box.

Storage of My Favorite Tapes

Some time ago, I began storing my most commonly used tapes in a small box. As I do my journaling, I reach for the tapes in this box first.

When I come across new favorites, I add those tapes to the box to replace the ones I no longer use as much. This organic style of organizing saves me a lot of time when I'm choosing tapes to use.

B.
The Storage of Seals

Wooden Seals

I have two Muji transparent acrylic cosmetics boxes for storing my collections of the wooden seals, three drawers for the top one and five drawers for the bottom one.

These two transparent boxes contain all of my wooden seals. I also keep the box on the desk, so it's easier to access when I write my journal. The height of the box is very suitable for seals. Because the boxes are transparent, I have a general idea where everything is, and it's all nice and neat. You also can classify the seals in each drawer so as to make it easier to find them. When there is extra space in the box, I will also include small things related to the seals, such as acrylic handles, small inkpads, and the like.

Transparent Stamps

Transparent stamps are more difficult to store than wooden seals. Because their sizes vary greatly, it's hard to create a uniform arrangement for transparent seals. In addition, some of them lose their adhesion after two or three uses. If they are not properly stored, their useful life will be greatly shortened.

I have tried many ways to store transparent stamps. Here I recommend two ways that make it easy to store and use them.

In the lower left picture is a Muji postcard and photo album where I've collected my transparent stamps. The album I use is 20 pages.

Because the stamp itself has a certain thickness, when 20 pages are packed with stamps, the album will be ready to explode; more than 20 pages is too much. This album can contain 2-4 sheets of stamps on one page, and basically, can accommodate most of the different-size stamps on the market. It's convenient for looking though the seals, just as in a photo album, to find the one I need. After use, wipe the seal clean and store it again. Such storage is not only neat and orderly, but also can extend the seal's service life. When some seals gradually lose their stickiness, they can be stored in an album separately.

The below right picture is a Muji double-hole folder for collecting transparent stamps. The folder I use is B5 size. This collection tool is suitable for newly purchased stamps and stamps that are not used frequently. I will punch two holes on each sheet of transparent stamps and put them into the folder one by one. Select the appropriate seals for use, then wipe and re-paste them to the board after use.

// Seals in a Muji postcard and photo album

// Seals in a Muji two-hold holder

C.
The Storage of Notebooks

Frequently Used Notebooks

I put frequently used notebooks in the most accessible places, usually in the cart beside the desk. I put notebooks and their inserts on a shelf on my desk. When I'm ready to journal, I can simply reach for them.

I put my notebooks with leather covers in a box on my rolling storage shelf. That way they are close at hand when I'm ready to work in them, and very convenient. The leather covers are somewhat delicate, and keeping these journals boxed on the rolling storage shelf helps to keep them from getting scratched or dirty.

// In this picture are the notebooks and inserts I keep on a shelf on my desk.

// I keep leather covered notebooks in a box on the rolling storage shelf.

Less-Commonly-Used, New, and Full Notebooks

I keep less-commonly-used, new, and filled notebooks in a cabinet to keep them clean.

// Here are the notebooks I keep in the cabinet.

D.
The Storage of Pens

I store my pens in a variety of pen holders and keep commonly used pens, pencils and watercolor brushes on the shelf of my desk.

The rolling storage shelf is equipped with watercolor brush pens, soft-head pens, and markers of various colors. I use the materials on my desk more than the materials in the rolling storage.

// I keep cups and jars on my desk for holding all kinds of pens.

// I store additional pens and markers in the top drawer of my rolling storage shelf.

E.
The Storage of Ink

My commonly used inks are placed on the shelf of the desk, especially black and brown inks. When a pen runs out of ink, I can fill it directly at the desk. Unusual inks are put in another drawer to protect them from dust or breakage.

// Here are a few bottles of ink on my desk.

// Storing lesser used inks in a drawer keeps them safe from tipping over or breaking.

F.
The Storage of Sticky Notes and Sticky Tabs

I collect sticky notes in one printed tin box, and sticky tabs in another. I keep these two boxes on the second level of the rolling storage shelf so they're easy to reach for when I need them.

// The sticky notes and tabs I collect.

// The sticky notes and tabs are collected in the second drawer of the rolling storage shelf.

G.
The Storage of Stickers

I use the vertical expanding bag to collect larger, unused stickers. It is easy to find stickers by labeling the expanding bag and sorting them in it. For loose stickers, I use smaller and transparent pockets to collect them, which makes it easy to find them. In addition, I use a card files to collect suitable size stickers.

1. Vertical expanding bag
2. Transparent storage bag
3. Transparent card file

// I classify the various graphic stickers roughly and put them in the transparent card file.

// I use blue storage bag strips to collect unopened sticker packs.

The Arrangement of My Journaling Corner

As a journaling lover who likes both shopping and tidiness, it is not enough to just tidy up my journaling stationery and materials. I also hope my room feels warm, neat, and orderly through proper organization.

I am someone who is too lazy to move when I am overwhelmed by a lot of things. But I love to tamper with the furnishings at home and change the position of furniture. Sometimes I rack my brains thinking of how to arrange the furnishings because there are too many things. It's also a pleasure for me. In the process of continuously storing, collating, and purchasing, I find that maximizing space is the most critical issue.

For someone who loves journaling, it's a great pleasure to have a desk that I can devote to it, and a cabinet where I can keep my books and stationery.

// Here is a table in the corner of my bedroom where I often lie back to write in a journal, read books, or sit in a trance.

01

Organizing Your Desk—Making Full Use of Desk Space

A.

Comparing the Pictures of My Desk in 2017 and 2018

// In 2017, there were just a few decorations and objects on my desk: A bunch of flowers, a picture, a lamp, some pens and colors.

// In 2018, my journaling supplies had increased, pushing me to redesign, and reuse the desk space. I added 10 lever arch files, a desk organizer, and a desk storage rack. There are some journals, two multilayer cosmetic boxes, and a Classiky wooden box on the rack. Behind the wooden box are several illustrated handbooks.

B.

Keeping All Sorts of Items but Leaving Some Space for Writing and Drawing

- Take advantage of space on top of desk

- Use your imagination and find creative ways to use organizers

- Arrange your supplies in a way that works for you and choose your favorite storage containers

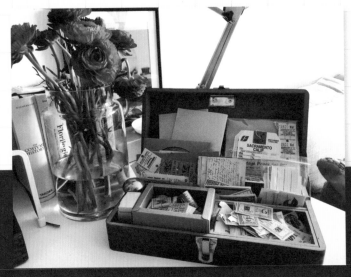

// I stack Lever Arch Files on the desk and put items on the top of them. To the right of the desk is a storage rack where I keep journals and seals above and my tape box and other items below.

// This is a Classiky wooden box, my favorite decorative storage box. I put it at an angle on the corner of my desk with a lamp as the background, to make the space less crowded and cramped.

// This is a 3-layer circular rotating organizer which used to be a skincare product storage shelf. I find it also can store penholders, ink bottles, and other small items, so I moved the organizer to my desk.

// The organizer has three layers: I keep penholders and ink bottles in the bottom layer, and ink bottles in the bottom layer, my frequently used inkpads and folders in the middle layer, and some smaller items in the top layer. It is multi-functional and practical for storage.

// The white rack beside the organizer was originally used on top of the microwave oven in the kitchen. Now I keep it on my desk.

02
Rolling Storage Shelf

// There is a rolling storage shelf beside my desk. It is stuffed with my frequently used items which fail to find a place on the desk. I keep the rolling storage shelf close at hand to get items easily. They are arranged in order of their use: the lower things are placed, the less frequently they are used.

// In the top layer, I keep some penholders packed with watercolor brush pens, marker pens, and brush pens. Next to the penholders there are tapes, hole punches, and other small things in a plastic container with dividers.

// I keep a box of notebooks, a box of sticky notes, a box of sticky tabs, and some boxes of number seals in the middle layer.

// In the bottom layer, I keep some big boxes of Cavallini seals and a transparent container packed with some craft supplies such as inkpads, embossing powder, paste, and string.

03
Cabinet Under Desk

// Don't neglect the space under your desk. Here I I've stored a transparent plastic cabinet for keeping less-commonly-used items.

// Some items that are hard to categorize can also go into the cabinet, like staples, plates, embossers, sealing wax, and other stationery items.

// This drawer contains a lot of dot liners.

// This drawer contains all kinds of ink.

04

Lots of Different Bookshelves Stuffed with Books

There are many books in my room. Over the years, as I have bought books, I've also bought shelves.

// I bought these three bookshelves successively over three years. The brown one in the middle is my favorite bookshelf from Muji made of recycled cardboard. It is very light without books and solid with five shelves packed with books. This bookshelf is cost-effective for its high storage capacity.

// I bought this white bookshelf at Ikea. On the bottom shelf I store four boxes of printing and watercolor paper.

// These floating shelves in my bedroom were already in place when I moved into this apartment. Now they are stuffed with books.

Economical and Environment-Friendly Containers

I see all kinds of boxes, tins, and trays being tossed out all the time. In fact, many of my containers are directly from the waste bin.

I have always thought that the container itself is also an item that needs to be contained. So the more containers you buy, the heavier burden you have. I have a knack for finding containers that had other purposes in my life and recycling them as containers for holding my journaling supplies—turning waste to my advantage. It's always a happy surprise.

// This is an instant drip coffee box. When the box was empty, I put my materials cut from paper in it. The divider in the middle of box helps me organize the materials into two groups.

01

How I Take Advance of Waste in My Life

A.

The Boxes Easily Ignored in Life

A lot of ready-made boxes perfect for keeping journaling items are waiting for your discovery.

1. **Delivery box**
2. **Candy box**
3. **Hobochini page-a-day planner box**
4. **Small white box**

// I store tapes in a candy box whose size and divider are perfect for the tapes. They fill the box without leaving any excessive space and they are held in place by the divider. The small white box in the upper right, is used for holding small stickers.

B.
Don't Throw away These "Penholders"

I washed the scented candle jar after use and kept it as a penholder along with other small jars and cups. They add a decorative touch to the desk.

// What are now penholders used to be scented candle jars and water bottles.

C.

Any Tray Can Be a Container for Journaling Items

Whether it's an ornamental iron tray or a fruit tray, I'll use it as a journaling item tray.

// I have a habit of choosing tapes and materials first and figuring out how to use them in my journaling collages later. Thus these two trays serve as containers for my tapes and materials. Compared with boxes, they have a larger surface and accommodate more tapes and materials.

D.

Cheap Office Supplies

The small storage bags that I keep in my binder were once used for keeping value-added tax (VAT) invoices. They are cheap and are just the right size for holding leftover bits and pieces.

// In the binder, small bags store leftover bits and pieces.

02

How to Make a Desk Storage Box with a Divider

The steps for a box with two cells

Tools: 1. a box with a cover 2. ruler 3. pencil 4. scissors

// Draw a line down the middle of the bottom of the box with a pencil and ruler. Use scissors to cut along the line.

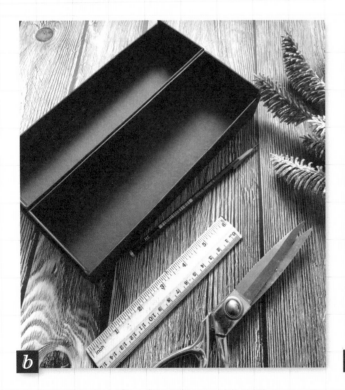

// Turn the box halves right side up and place them inside the lid. Now the box is divided in two.

// The tapes are presented in the vertical bar space.

The steps for a box with four cells

// Cut the box into four pieces along horizontal and vertical lines.

// Put the four corners of the box together as shown.

// Set the dividers into the box cover. The box with four cells is done.

// This type of box is suitable for storage of bottles, such as ink bottles.

Section 02

"JOURNALING ATTITUDES" IN LIFE

The essence of journaling is to record traces of life so "journaling attitudes" touch every aspect of my life. This little fact has sunk into me by osmosis and influences my behavior.

Whether I am staying at home, going out with friends, celebrating various festivals, birthdays, and seasons, reading, doing sports, or traveling, I am always affected by my "journaling attitudes".

"Journaling Attitudes" Displayed in Room

In fact, journaling represents a positive outlook on life. The sensible and cozy arrangement in room should be a "journaling attitude" I expect.

In usual journaling, I mostly enjoy the light-hearted atmosphere spread in the entire room: I sit among stationery and materials, opening the notebook, writing down the interesting things, lighting the scented candles, occasionally mediating and flicking through some pages of new illustrated handbook. All these scenes make me smile instinctively. So I make my room very seriously. In addition to the orderly storage and arrangement, I would often add decorations and plant, changing the configuration of the room irregularly with the season and mood.

01

Desk Arrangement and Wall Decoration in Different Periods

My desk is where I spend most of my time doing journaling. I redecorate the wall in front of my desk every once in a while.

In recent years, I've changed the style of my desk frequently. I also change the decoration on my desk wall frequently, according to my current preferences for looks and practicality. Sometimes I like things stark and minimal, sometimes I like the wall filled to the max. Sometimes, when I have a lot of things to store, the desk is stacked high with boxes.

// My desk in different periods

02

How I Commonly Arrange and Decorate My Desk and Wall

A.

Wire Wall Grid Panel

It is practical and attractive to hang a wire grid panel on the wall. I have a tendency to keep my personal accessories randomly on the wire grid so that the wall seems light-hearted and casual. The wire grid is usually hung with my small watercolor paintings, postcards from my friends, birthday cards, and sometimes one or two string pendants.

B.

White Wooden Boxes

This is white wooden box that I bought in 2016. I keep small seals and clips in the box. On top of it are my commonly-used scented candles and a few small decorations. A wooden storage box is a good-looking and practical item combined with other desk storage items.

C.
Desk Calendar and Wall Calendar

In 2018, my wall was hung with a weekly calendar, one week per page.

I highlighted each important date as a reminder. It is also a good idea to keep a calendar on the desk and write down the to-do list for each day as a reminder.

Desk calendars and wall calendars provide a kind of ritual; turning the pages reminds us to cherish every moment.

D.
Scented Candle Holder

I have many aromatherapy cups. When I draw and write at my desk, I like to light them. Putting several commonly used scented candle holders on the desk, makes them convenient to use and adds a few decorative touches. But paper products should be kept as far away from the flame as possible. For safety, I keep them on top of the storage box.

03
Decorations to Make the Room Cozy

A.
Vigorous Plants

Setting out one or two pots of green plants or a vase of flowers can liven up the space. The fresh flowers delight me when I go home. Plants reflect the change of season and let me know when I should change my arrangements to suit the time of year. If the life of flowers is too short for you, go with plants instead.

B.
Your Hand-Painted Decorations

Ever since I learned watercolor, I've mounted and framed my best paintings and drawings and displayed them in my room. I frame the smaller paintings with ready-made frames and hang them up or keep them on my desk. I bring larger paintings to a professional framer, and then hang the finished works on my walls. I also use tape to attach unframed pictures to my walls—which are gradually being covered! Looking at them gives my heart a wonderful sense of accomplishment.

04
Arranging Festive Decorations

Setting out a few holiday decorations can instantly give a room a festive atmosphere.

There are many decorations for Christmas: Wax-sealed berry candle holders, Christmas dolls, flower wreaths and deer ornaments. Arranging small items in my room makes me feel the approaching festival.

"Journaling Attitudes" in Social Life

"Journaling attitudes" are also fully reflected in my daily social life. Under my influence, many of my friends have gotten into journaling. My gifts to friends are mostly stationery items wrapped by myself. I'm in the habit of collecting and mailing local postcards when I travel, and make greeting cards for friends' birthdays. In the process, I have made acquaintances, participated in various journaling activities, and attended sharing meetings... I think these unexpected pleasures have come to me because of journaling.

01

DIY Birthday Card to Friend

A greeting card that you make yourself or your family or friends is a fulfilling and precious gift. It also represents an expression of your good will.

// This is a birthday card I made for my close friend. I decorated it with watercolor and English handwriting.

// A bow with pink ribbon tied on the envelope is sealed with golden sealing wax. My friend loves it so much that it is still displayed on her bookshelf.

02

Postcards Collected on Travels

When I travel I collect all kinds of local postcards and send them to my friends whenever I can. Postcards allow me to share my thoughts with them as I travel. I collect postcards from places I visit as souvenirs.

// The postcard that I bought in the YSL garden in Morocco shares the same shooting angle as the background. It is quite unique.

// The postcards I collected on my travels.

03

Gift Exchanges of Journaling Friends

We journaling buddies often mail journaling stationery to each other. Every gift I receive is packaged exquisitely.

// My friend MOMO QIN sent me some stickers and post-it notes. She made special package for every item.

// This DIY collage postcard by MOMO QIN is quietly vintage and delicate.

04
Beautiful DIY Gift Packaging

I like giving my family and friends beautifully wrapped presents so that they feel my special intentions when they receive their gifts.

There are so many materials for gift packaging, which can be selected according to the style, age, personality, and hobby of the gift recipients. When giving gifts to my peers, I like to wrap them in kraft paper with hemp string and leaves and cards as decorations, and I sometimes seal them with sealing wax. When I give gifts to my elders, I choose delicate wrapping paper with ribbons as decorations.

// A few of my special gift wraps

A.
The Simple Steps for Gift Packaging

1. Wrapping paper
2. Gift box
3. Scissors
4. Double-sided tape
5. Ribbon

a

// First, apply tape to the edge of the box.

b

// Wrap the box with wrapping paper, and press the paper to show the imprints of the corner and edges of the box. Remove the backing paper from a strip of double-sided tape, insert it along the inside of the overlapped edge, and apply pressure.

c

// Fold the excess paper on the ends toward the inside of the box.

d

// Apply double-sided tape as shown. Fold the end up, and press it into place.

// Here is another way to fold and attach the ends. Fold the excess paper inward as before, forming two triangles. Fold the top triangle toward box.

// Fold in the tip of the triangle to create a blunt edge. The folded edge should coincide with the vertical edge of the box.

// Apply two tape strips as shown.

// Your wrapped box is complete.

// Cross the ribbons on the box, and keep the ribbon flat. The picture shows the bottom of the box. Don't make a dead knot where it crosses, and be sure the ribbon is crossed.

// Turn the box right-side up and cross the ribbon on top. Make a firm knot in the middle.

k

l

// Tie the ribbon into a bow in the middle and make the ribbon fluffy.

// Cut off the excess ribbon. The decoration of the package is done.

m

FUTURE COLLABORATIONS

If you wish to participate in SendPoints' future projects and publications, please send your website or portfolio to editor01@sendpoints.cn.